Lennie

The Autobiography of
LENNIE LAWRENCE
With Kevin Brennan

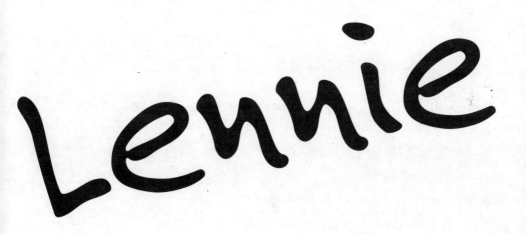

Foreword by Sir Alex Ferguson

GreenUmbrella Publishing

This edition first published in the UK in 2009
By Green Umbrella Publishing

© Green Umbrella Publishing 2009

www.gupublishing.co.uk

Publishers Jules Gammond and Vanessa Gardner

Creative Director: Kevin Gardner

Printed and bound by J F Print Ltd., Sparkford, Somerset

ISBN: 978-1-906635-90-9

To Jenny (Duckie), my partner, soul-mate and a massive influence on my personal and professional life. Lots of people go through their lives without ever meeting the right person, that hasn't happened to me and I realise just how lucky I am to have found her.

I also want to dedicate this book to my late parents, Jack and Ethel, my brother David, his wife Shirley, and my cousin Pauline and her husband Peter as well as Jenny's family, especially her mum and dad, Bertha and Willie.

Lennie Lawrence

CONTENTS

FOREWORD

I first met Lennie back in the 1980's when he was a frequent visitor to Scotland. At the time I was manager of Aberdeen and he was in charge of Charlton Athletic. He was always travelling north to watch matches and probably knew more about Scottish players than most other English managers.

Over a period of time we got to know each other pretty well and when I moved to England to become manager of Manchester United we continued our friendship. What he achieved in the mid-1980's with Charlton was quite remarkable, as he put together a promotion winning team despite a real lack of financial resources and the club having to move away from The Valley to use Crystal Palace's Selhurst Park ground as their 'home'. All of this came after the club had almost gone out of existence, and I know that as a relatively young and inexperienced manager at the time, Lennie showed great leadership qualities to help steer Charlton through some troubled times.

Perhaps his greatest achievement came following that promotion in 1986 to the old First Division when, against all the odds, he somehow managed to keep Charlton in the top flight of English football for four seasons. Lennie's name became synonymous with that of Charlton Athletic, and when he left to become manager of Middlesbrough in 1991, a lot of people were surprised that he chose to start again with another club after nine successful years in charge of Londoners.

Lennie went on to lead Boro to promotion from the Second Division, and since then has also had promotion success with the likes of Cardiff City and more recently with Bristol Rovers in his role as director of football with them. He has also coached or managed at Plymouth, Lincoln,

Bradford, Luton and Grimsby during a long and distinguished career which has seen him notch up more than 1,000 games as a manager. It is an achievement he can rightly be proud of and during all of that time Lennie has remained very much the same man I first met all those years ago back in Scotland.

It has been a pleasure to know him and to call him a friend. After a lifetime in the business which spans more than 30 years I know Lennie has a tale or two to tell. Like me he is very much a footballing man and I know that the story of his life will be read and enjoyed by anyone interested in the game we both love.

Lennie was always someone whom I could always phone when wanting to find out anything on players in the lower leagues, as his knowledge of these leagues was exceptional, and he would tell you himself I used to barrage him with phone calls at the beginning of the season to assess which teams he thought were going to do well and who the up and coming young players were, and sure as God he would be bang on.

Sir Alex Ferguson August 2009

Lennie Lawrence

1

TEN GOOD REASONS

I was in a complete daze as I drove around the M25. In less than the space of a week my whole life had changed and I was still trying to come to terms with exactly what had happened.

The news was out and I had been officially unveiled as the new manager of Middlesbrough earlier in the day. It seemed as though just about everyone I knew wanted to speak to me and my car phone was red hot with calls. I was driving home after some of the most hectic days I'd ever experienced and as I headed towards my house in Kent, it was almost as if I was on auto-pilot. I still couldn't quite get my head around what had gone on, but I knew I had to start getting used to the idea of not being the Charlton manager any more after nine incredible years with the club, and start thinking about the future at the other end of the country with Middlesbrough.

The experiences I'd had in my career up to that point had left me feeling as though I could cope with anything that was thrown at me, but I hadn't been prepared for what happened when I picked up the phone seven days earlier at my home to call the Middlesbrough chief executive Keith Lamb.

I wanted to talk to him about the possibility of sorting out a deal that would bring a player named Alan Kernaghan south to sign for Charlton. He'd played a huge part in helping the club stay up when he was with us on loan during the previous season and I was determined to make sure he signed on a permanent basis. Kernaghan was just the sort of centre-half I believed we needed to have at the club as I started to lay the groundwork for a new season. I'd even gone as far as meeting him in Barnsley during the summer, giving him 10 good reasons to move south and become a Charlton Athletic player.

After chatting through some of the details of a possible move and with the conversation centred on just what Charlton were prepared to pay for Kernaghan's services, Keith suddenly took the wind out of my sails.

"What about you Lennie?" he asked. "What's the situation with you and Charlton?"

It soon became pretty clear that he was asking whether I would be open to the possibility of finally moving on from Charlton. It took me a few seconds to come to terms with the way the conversation was going. I had loved my time at Charlton despite all the trials and tribulations. It was my club and I had become part of the fabric of the place. In many ways I'd never really had time to think about leaving.

But it was obvious Keith wasn't just asking out of idle curiosity. Middlesbrough were in the market for a new manager and suddenly I was the man they were after. Did I turn the idea down point blank, or offer the sort of encouragement that would lead to them taking the matter further? It didn't take me long to decide, and I told him I'd be interested in hearing what they had in mind.

I have to admit that I was flattered to be asked and it was a nice feeling to have another club clearly believing in you. Don't get me wrong, I loved Charlton and knew that whatever else happened in my career, they would always hold a special place in my affections because we had both been through such a lot together. During my time with them I had become part of the furniture in many people's eyes, and I'd probably experienced more in a nine year period than most managers have to cope with throughout their entire career.

I had seen highs and lows, all sorts of twists and turns and enough drama to have filled several scripts for any TV soap, but most of all I'd grown to love the club and its amazing supporters. We had all seen and done so much and during my time there Charlton Athletic had changed from being just another football club into becoming a cause. There was never really a dull moment from the very first day I took over. We had flirted with extinction, ground-shared with our biggest rivals and won promotion to the top flight of the English game, surviving against all the odds for four seasons before being relegated.

It had been impossible not to get caught up in the long and determined battle by the fans to help restore the club to its true home at The Valley. That battle had meant a financial drain on resources as the board tried to make sure the club would no longer have to ground share. It was without question the right thing to do, but from my point of view it also meant I had little or no money with which to build or strengthen the team. I had no problem with that and could fully understand what was happening, but when results are going badly it inevitably has an effect, not only on your league position, but also on morale. With a few exceptions here and there we had become a selling club, and everybody knew it.

After those unbelievable years in the top flight rubbing shoulders with the elite of the English game, reality had struck when we finally dropped out of the division. We had performed minor miracles to stay up there with the big boys and I think the Charlton fans realised that. In many ways they perhaps saw their time in the First Division as something of a bonus, and I think to many of them the real achievement was going to come when they could finally walk through the turnstiles at The Valley once again and celebrate the fact that the club was finally back at its rightful home.

At the time I doubt that many of those fans thought I would be the target for another club. I was viewed as 'Good Old Lennie,' the manager who had seen them through thick and thin. They'd even produced stickers with 'Lennie Is Our Leader' printed on them. Without realising it I had become more than just the manager at the club. We were all in it together, the board, the manager, the team and the fans. All fighting for the Charlton cause and despite having just experienced a disappointing season in what was then the Second Division, there seemed little chance of things changing on the management front.

Perhaps that's why the conversation with Keith Lamb surprised me so much. I had become so accustomed to being the manager of Charlton that even I had difficulty in thinking of myself going to another club. Middlesbrough clearly had other ideas. They had seen what I'd been able to do with little or no real money against the backdrop of all the problems off the field, and decided that with more cash and resources I might just be the man they were looking for.

They say things move fast in football and what had happened to me during the course of seven days certainly proved that point. I've always believed that everyone has five or six crossroads in their lives and I knew I had reached one of mine when I was asked whether I wanted to leave Charlton.

The club had given me my opportunity as a manager, and to this day they are a massive chunk of my life story, what I hadn't quite realised at the time was that Middlesbrough and the clubs that followed, would provide so many more new chapters for me.

2

WHAT'S IN A NAME?

Robin Michael Lawrence. No, that's not the name of my father, or my two brothers. It is, in fact, my name. Even though I've been known throughout my career as Lennie, my real name is Michael and I use it for any official documents and for things like writing cheques, but as far as anyone in the football world is concerned I am, and always will be, Lennie Lawrence.

I honestly can't remember when I was first called Lennie, but I think it was some time during my schooldays at John Ruskin Grammar in Croydon. Who used it and why? I really can't tell you, but the name stuck and I obviously very quickly got used to it because everyone I knew, with the exception of my family, called me by the name. Maybe Lennie Lawrence had a ring to it that I liked, whatever it was I never made any great effort to stop people using it and I've been comfortable with the name ever since.

I went to John Ruskin after moving to Croydon from Brighton with my family after my dad, Jack, who was a civil servant, got a new job there, and the family followed and relocated to the area. It really doesn't seem that far these days, but back then I suppose it was a bit of an upheaval for all of us and instead of the south coast that we'd become accustomed to, we were suddenly much closer to London. I'd been born in Brighton in December 1947 and had lived the early part of my childhood there along with my mum, Ethel, and two brothers, David and John. I was the oldest of the three kids with David second in line a few years younger than me and John a couple of years younger than him. David showed some real sporting skill as a kid and went on to become the British lightweight judo champion, only just missing out on a place in the Olympic squad for the 1972 games in Munich. It was a pretty happy and contented childhood and although I was always interested in football, I couldn't claim that I was ever mad about the game. It was something I was interested in along with the usual pursuits a boy has, but obviously as I grew older it began to play a more important role in my life.

Dad was never a supporter of a particular football team and over the years he took me to see a variety of sides, which was great from my point of view and I had a great time just going to watch very good matches and some very good players. My memory isn't great when it comes to recalling all of those times, but I do remember three games in particular that stick in my mind. The first was being taken to see Brighton play a pre-season friendly at the old Goldstone Ground when we still lived in the area, and they won 6-0 in front of a big crowd. The other two came later on in my teens when we'd moved to Croydon and by that time we tended to go to most of the London grounds, because they were easier to get to and there were also a lot of teams to choose from. One Saturday afternoon my dad took me to Stamford Bridge to watch Chelsea play. I can honestly say that I haven't got a clue who they were playing that day, because the biggest memory I have was the fact that the crowd was so huge. There must have been more than 60,000 in the ground and, of course, in those days most of the people attending matches stood on the terraces. I was lifted up to a place at the back of the stands from where I could just about see the pitch, but I don't think my dad or a lot of the other supporters in front of me knew much about what was going on, because they could hardly see the pitch. They had to rely on the cheers and shouts from the crowd to keep them up to date with the action.

On another occasion we went along to North London and I was

lucky enough to see the great Stanley Matthews play against Arsenal at Highbury. It was a terrific afternoon for someone like me, because by this time I was starting to show a bit of talent when it came to playing football at schoolboy level, and enjoyed turning out for John Ruskin and for the district team.

Because I went to a grammar school our football was structured a bit differently to a lot of other schools. For some reason most of our fixtures were friendly matches against other grammar schools, but the opposition got a lot broader when it came to Cup competitions. Schoolboy football was a big thing back then and we'd often travel to fixtures with several teams, from the first 11 right down to the kids who were in the youngest age category at the school. It was all taken very seriously and the whole operation was well planned and controlled each week.

When I got to first team level I found myself in the company of some pretty useful footballers, and there was nobody better than a little kid who was a bit younger than me, he seemed to be able to score goals for fun at whatever level he played at. He was so much better than any of the rest of us and you didn't have to be an expert to realise he was destined to earn his living from the professional game. His name was Steve Kember and he went on to make a big name for himself as a midfielder, first with local club, Crystal Palace, and then with Chelsea. He also had spells managing Palace after his playing career came to an end.

Two other boys at the school were also pretty useful players, although neither of them were in Steve's league on the pitch. Their names were Roy Hodgson and Bobby Houghton, both went on to earn money playing, but it was as coaches and managers that they really went on to shine in the professional game. Roy managed several teams abroad including Inter Milan and of course was in charge of Blackburn Rovers for a time, and is rightly recognised as one of the best and most knowledgeable coaches in the game. He's now the manager of Fulham and has done a superb job with them. When he first took over they were looking doomed to relegation from the Premier League, but he has turned the whole thing around and last season guided then to a place in Europe, which is a tremendous achievement.

Bobby also went on to earn fame and fortune abroad, and like Roy he has also managed in the English leagues, but perhaps one of his most striking achievements was managing to get Swedish side, Malmo, to the European Cup final in 1979 where they lost to Nottingham Forest by the only goal of the game scored by Trevor Francis. As things were to turn out, both Roy and Bobby went on to spend a large part of their careers abroad, while I ended up spending mine criss-crossing the motorways of England!

I can't say, hand-on-heart, whether the four of us all played in the same school team together at the same time, but we were certainly all at the school and got on well with each other. We still do to this day and over the years I've always kept in touch with Roy and Bobby. Both perhaps had more of an influence on my eventual career, because I saw them go off and start coaching which was something we were all passionate about from a very early age. But there was no way back then that any of us thought we would all go on to be managers in the professional English game. I doubt there can be many schools who can boast of having four pupils in their ranks who would go on to be football managers.

Although I loved football I very quickly realised there was no way I was going to be good enough to go on and earn a living from playing the game. I did have a short spell training with Crystal Palace but unlike Steve who was signed by them at the age of 15, I didn't have an exceptional talent. I was a hard-working midfielder, and then a defender, who tried to make the most of what talent I had. It was enough to make me a very decent schoolboy player and a few years later I was able to go on and play in non-league football with Croydon and then Carshalton, but that was always going to be the limit for me on the pitch.

What I did begin to realise was that I had a real passion for coaching, and I knew that was what I wanted to do. I was realistic and honest enough with myself to know that I was never going to make my mark as a player, but I genuinely felt I might have some talent as a coach and that's where I began to direct my thoughts and plans.

After leaving school I wasn't at all sure what I was going to do. I left with a couple of A-levels, but instead of going on to further education, I decided that I'd go out and earn myself some money for a year, and ended up doing a variety of jobs including working in insurance for a time. What I was sure about was the fact that I wanted to continue my football education and I did this by taking my FA preliminary badge at the age of just 19, and was lucky enough to have Bobby Robson as one of the people on the staff for some of the course. It was very clear that coaching was something I really found interesting and I also became involved in the Surrey coaches association, going along to various courses and sessions with Roy, Bobby and another great friend of ours called Colin Toal.

After my year of working for a living I decided that going to college would be a better long-term move for me and I went up to the Midlands for three years to study at The City of Birmingham College of Education, doing a physical education course with history as a second subject. I enjoyed it and thought it would at least give me some sort of base with which to start a career. I knew I wanted to coach but at that time the idea of working full-time in the professional game wasn't really on. Instead, I was able to combine the course with returning home now and again to keep up with my coaching on a practical level by taking sessions involving kids from the local Croydon area during school holidays and sometimes at weekends.

By this time both Roy and Bobby had taken the first steps in what were to be very distinguished careers managing and coaching abroad, with both of them working in Sweden. I was taking a slightly different route and when I finished my course in Birmingham I got a job as part of the PE department at Malory school in South London, combining my teaching duties with playing non-league football as a defender with Croydon and then Carshalton Athletic.

It was quite an enjoyable life for me at the time, combining my teaching with playing non-league football, but during the mid 1970's I got the opportunity to start doing some coaching at Carshalton, thanks to the manager Phil Amato, and took to it like a duck to water. Once I knew I could coach at that level, I very quickly realised I wanted to make the step up to the full-time game, but I was also realistic enough to know that it wouldn't be easy. Most people who coached or managed in the professional game had also played at that level as well, which put me at a distinct disadvantage.

What I did have going for me was the fact that I had made quite a few contacts over the years taking part in various FA courses, and one of those contacts was someone called Mike Kelly. I had told him once that if he ever heard about the possibility of a job with a league club, I'd be grateful if he could let me know about it because I really fancied having a crack at coaching on a full-time basis. It wasn't arrogance because I've always been very realistic about what I can and can't do. I think it was in my nature to try and go for something like that. I could easily have carried on with a very comfortable lifestyle, teaching and coaching in the non-league game, but with me it's usually a case of all or nothing, and I was sure that I wanted to immerse myself in coaching. It was simply a case of me knowing that I was good enough to make that next step, but as is so often the case, it's getting the opportunity that can be the hardest part of the equation.

At the time, Mike was the reserve team manager at Plymouth Argyle, but in 1977 Tony Waiters, who like Mike had been a goalkeeper in his playing days, left the club. They gave Mike the chance to take over as manager and I got a call from him one day saying they were looking to get someone in to take charge of the reserves. Was I interested? Mike didn't have to ask twice. I would have walked all the way to Devon for the chance to take over his old job, but it wasn't quite as straight forward as that because I was told that there was someone else in for the position and the club wanted to hold interviews. I went down and had mine with Mike and the Plymouth chairman Robert Daniel. The interview went well and I felt confident about my chances when I came out of it. Happily, I didn't have to wait too long to have that fact confirmed, because they offered me the chance to realise my dream.

So, thanks to Mike, at the age of 29 I was up and running as a coach with a professional football team. I'd got the chance I wanted and I was determined to make the most of it.

3

WAY OUT WEST

After the euphoria of finally getting the chance to be a full-time coach with a professional football club, I very soon had to get to grips with some of the realities of my new job.

If you've played 500 games as a professional and got 50 caps you start a job as a coach or manager with the players giving you immediate respect, simply because of your record. In my case the players at Plymouth didn't really have a clue who I was. What they did know was that I'd never played professionally and also that I was probably younger than some of the more experienced members of the squad.

It was my job to coach the reserves and there was a bit of a mixture when it came to the type of players I was dealing with. I had young lads who had their careers in front of them, and some old pro's in the group who had fallen out of favour and weren't getting a look-in at first team level. What I knew I had to do right away was earn their respect and let them see that I could coach and do something for their game. I can't honestly remember my first day with any great detail, but I do recall I came off the training pitch feeling as though I'd done okay and that I was off and running.

Mike was an extremely good coach and it was really useful for me to be able to watch him on the training pitch and pick up some tips just by observing and seeing the way he went about his job. I very quickly began to settle into life at Plymouth. It was a good club with a very passionate support. The one drawback was probably the fact that it was so very far away from most other football clubs, and any match we played was always a real trek.

I wasn't on my own when I moved down from London, because my girlfriend at the time decided she would come with me. Her name was Avril, and I'd been seeing her for a while. I suppose it was a real change of lifestyle and environment for both of us, but we enjoyed the place and I was obviously delighted to be coaching each day, working with players and taking charge of the reserve team. Things went well for me and Mike was good to work for, but the first team failed to make a real impact in the league and we were never one of the challengers in what was then the old Third Division. After a 3-0 defeat at Cambridge United in February 1978, the first team found themselves in 21st place in the league and a few days later Mike Kelly resigned as the manager.

The club didn't exactly have a big staff but they needed someone to step in and take over. So at the tender age of 30, and with only about six months experience in the professional game, I found myself in temporary charge when Plymouth decided to make me their caretaker manager. It wasn't something I had too much time to ponder over because I was appointed the day after Mike left the club, and in my first game in charge 10 days later, we earned a very decent 1-1 draw at Gillingham, who were top of the league at the time, with a goal from Gary Megson.

It was a good result and in all I had five games in charge drawing three and losing the other two. My last game came against Lincoln at home and we lost it 2-1. That match was on a Monday night and by the Thursday of that same week the club had appointed a familiar figure as their new manager, with the return to Plymouth of Malcolm Allison, 13 years after he was last in charge at the club.

On the day he was appointed I drove like a maniac to be at a meeting with him and the chairman, wheeling in and out of traffic as if I was in some kind of race. I wanted to make sure I got there on time and needed to find out exactly what was going to happen to me.

Malcolm was a big figure in the game with a huge reputation, and was a larger-than-life personality. I didn't know him, but like everyone else, I knew of him and he was reckoned by many to be one of the best coaches in the game. He'd also become nationally known over the years because of his appearances on the box as a TV pundit. I wasn't sure whether he would want me around, and certainly didn't know what to expect when I first met him, but he was really good about the situation I found myself in and made it clear he wanted me to stay on and help him in much the same way as I had assisted Mike.

We got on fine and although I would never claim that we were bosom buddies, we certainly had a very good working relationship and it was a great learning experience for me to be on the same training ground with Malcolm. He was always trying to be innovative and different. I wouldn't say he was a great manager and I don't think I learnt much from him in that respect, but he was an extremely good coach and worked well with players. He loved being out there each day and working on new ideas.

With all due respect to the lads who were in the squad at the time, they were in the Third Division and not the First, but that didn't stop Malcolm from trying to get them playing attractive football that was often very different to the way they had been asked to play in the past.

I remember once seeing the team look totally bemused when Malcolm announced how he was intending to set them up for the next game. He basically told them they were going to be playing with a sweeper, some wide overlapping full-backs, but no centre-forward. The players clearly thought they hadn't heard him correctly, but they had and that's the way the team went out and lined up the following Saturday.

It didn't always work but at the same time it was a hugely enjoyable experience for me, even though he tended to do most of the coaching. That was fine by me, because once again it gave me the chance to observe and learn. When you see another coach in action it's not a case of just going away and slavishly copying them when you next take a session, but at the same time it is an opportunity to maybe take some of the things you've seen and mould them into what you are trying to do with players on different occasions. Malcolm had a presence and a way of doing things that I think made him unique. He loved to tinker with systems and was very good when it came to set-plays.

We were never really able to pull ourselves clear of the relegation zone and the thought of the drop was hanging over us as we went into the last few games of the season. In our third from last game we played at Shrewsbury and lost 3-1. It put a lot of pressure on us for the last two matches which were both at home, but we managed to win them, beating Port Vale 3-2 and then thrashing Bradford 6-0 three days later to finish the season in 19th place.

It had been quite an introduction to full-time professional football for me during that first season, and I soon realised how quickly things can change for you. In theory I could have been out on my ear very quickly if Malcolm hadn't fancied keeping me at the club, and with very little experience under my belt, who knows what might have happened. Instead, I'd worked alongside two outstanding coaches and even had a taste of being a manager in the Football League – all in less than a year!

Despite the precarious nature of the job I was more convinced than ever that I'd done the right thing and knew that a life in football was exactly what I wanted. Pre-season training went well that summer and we made a decent start to the campaign. By October we were fourth in the table and it looked as though we could be on course for a possible promotion challenge.

We dipped a little towards the end of the year and by the time the Christmas period came around we were in a mid-table position, and the first team hadn't managed a win since the middle of November. Malcolm was still very much in charge, but rumours had started speculating about a possible move by Manchester City to take him back to the club he'd enjoyed great success with during an earlier period in the north. It soon became obvious the rumours were true, and it seemed to a lot of people that it would just be a matter of time before the Maine Road club came calling for his services.

I actually asked Malcolm what he would do if the move to City didn't come off, because it was obviously a great job and he knew it would put him back in the big time where a character like him clearly belonged. I'm sure he must have been desperate for the whole thing to happen, but you would never have really guessed it by the way he went about things on a daily basis. He just got on with the job of coaching the players and managed to put all the speculation to the back of his mind. When I spoke to him about it he just shrugged his shoulders and said if it didn't come off he'd just get on with his job at Plymouth, and I'm sure that's exactly what he would have done. He seemed able to just focus on whatever life brought his way and get on with it. As things turned out City did ask Malcolm to return to the club early in January 1979, and I don't think there was ever any doubt about him refusing their offer, and very soon he was heading north to take up his new job where initially he was known as their 'coaching overlord'.

It wasn't all bad for Plymouth either, because although they had lost their manager, they were reportedly paid something like £35,000 by City in compensation. As for me it was the end of a short but enjoyable experience working with, and getting to know, one of the game's great coaches and characters. To this day I still have nothing but respect for

Malcolm and the way he was able to bring a real freshness and feeling of anticipation to the training pitch on a daily basis.

I can also remember how generous he could be as a person. I went to his wedding during the time he was at Plymouth, and after the ceremony in Kent we all went out for a great evening that ended in a West End club with Malcolm paying for everything and acting as the perfect host.

He loved life and lived it to the full, he also loved his football and ultimately he was a genuinely nice guy and it was a privilege to work alongside him. Years later when I was manager of Middlesbrough I got a phone call in my office one morning. Malcolm was on the other end of the line asking me if there was any chance of him coming to work with me in some capacity. Middlesbrough had been another club he'd managed in his career, and he was in charge at Ayresome Park early in the 1980's. There really wasn't anything I could do for him, because I already had people in place and I also felt it would never have worked. As far as I was concerned he was a number one, or in other words, someone who should be in charge. I didn't really feel any other role would have worked for him or for me, but I still regret the fact that I wasn't able to do anything for him at the time.

When Malcolm left it was the second time in less than two years that I'd experienced a managerial change at the club, and I was rapidly being initiated into the ways of the professional game when it came to football management. The old saying about the only certain thing when you become a manager is that one day you will get the sack was obviously very true.

I'd been fortunate when Mike Kelly left because Malcolm was happy to have me stay at the club and work with him, but my luck ran out second time around and I suddenly got a taste of the knock-on effect there can be when a manager leaves a club for whatever reason. In fact, Malcolm leaving and going back to City changed the lives of all sorts of people at each club. There were lots of comings and goings and the local paper actually did an article on the effect his move had.

On a personal level the club said they would like me to stay on, but the new manager, Bobby Saxton, had other ideas. Like most managers Bobby had his own people that he wanted to work with and that meant there was no room for me. The club were very fair about it and I understood the situation, but it still left me looking for a job in a very uncertain profession and I didn't really know where I could look for work, only that I needed to get back to coaching as soon as I could.

Once again one of the contacts I'd made through coaching gave me the chance to get back into work very quickly, and within a matter of weeks I was moving from the south west and crossing the county to take up a coaching job with Colin Murphy at Lincoln City.

I was actually only out of work for about three weeks before I got the phone-call from Colin asking me if I wanted to join him at the club, and it turned out to be a fantastic experience for me. It was exactly what I needed and allowed me to experience just what running a football club was all about. During my time there I did just about every job and it knocked all the rough edges off of me. Murph was another one of the game's characters and he later got a bit of a reputation as one of football's eccentrics, but what he was first and foremost was a really good coach and someone with a fantastic eye for a player.

He had the ability to spot the potential in players from non-league teams and others who might not have done too well at other clubs, but he saw something in them and had a lot of success doing that during his time at Lincoln, not just when I was there, but also after I left them in 1982. For instance, he saw something in a tall gangling kid that nobody else was able to spot and the lad went on to have a pretty decent career in the game – his name was John Fashanu.

Colin loved getting the best out of the players he had and once again it was good for me to be around someone who could show me the ropes and also get me involved on all sorts of levels at the club. Lincoln were not exactly awash with money or star names, but it was a great place for me to really get stuck in and learn from the experience. He taught me an awful lot about management during my time there and opened my eyes to a lot of things.

Although that first season didn't go too well with the club getting relegated to the Fourth Division, we came straight back up the next season and were lucky enough to have a good group of players to work with. Two of them, Steve Thompson and George Shipley were to figure prominently in my career a few years later, and the group also had some strong characters, which is something I've always looked for over the years when I have been putting a squad together.

In all I spent three and a half years at the club and I will always look back on that time with great affection in the knowledge that it really helped set me up for a career in management. When I first went there I think at the back of my mind I thought I was ready to be a manager if the opportunity ever arose having had that brief encounter with the job at Plymouth, but I very quickly realised that wasn't the case and through working alongside Colin I was able to absorb a hell of a lot and get to know exactly what football management entailed.

He was happy to delegate responsibility and let me get on with things, which in turn meant that I was exposed to a hell of a lot during my time with him. For example, on transfer deadline day in March 1982, Murph called me in and said he wanted me to take care of some business for him. The result was that I was sent over to Scunthorpe to sort out the transfer of Steve Cammack from us to them, and in turn we were going to get

David Hughes from Scunthorpe. There was also the little matter of John Ward joining Lincoln from Grimsby that same afternoon. I had to wheel and deal all day as the transfers were sorted out and with 20 minutes to go before the deadline, I still had John sitting in his car with his transfer papers. There were no mobile phones, emails or faxes involved and in the end I had to make a call from a public phone box to make sure all the deals went through on time and were registered. It was hectic but I loved it and at the end of the day I knew I'd picked up another chunk of invaluable management experience.

At the end of the 1981-82 season Lincoln just missed out on promotion from the Third Division when they drew the last game of the season 0-0 at Fulham and finished fourth in the table. Promotion would have put them in what is now the Championship and it would have been a real achievement for a club of their size. Missing out meant the board had a bit of a think about the way they wanted things run and that in turn meant areas within the club like the youth policy were going to suffer. I was 34 and decided that it would be better for me to leave and look for something else. So I negotiated a deal with the club, getting myself a bit of money but with no idea of where my next job would be. You do that sort of thing when you're younger, but of course it was a real risk and it could have meant being out of work for a long time.

As things turned out it wasn't long before I was in work again at the start of what was to prove to be the most amazing nine years of my footballing life.

4

EXPRESS DELIVERY

When it comes to my newspaper each morning I have to admit I've always been a creature of habit. I don't quite know why but for years I have always bought a copy of the *Daily Mail*.

One morning shortly after packing in my job with Lincoln I went to the local newsagents for my paper only to find that they didn't have any copies of the *Mail*, so I bought the *Daily Express* instead. As usual I went straight to the back pages and sitting at the foot of one of them was an advert for a reserve team coach at Charlton Athletic. They'd had a bit of a turnaround during the summer with Alan Mullery leaving to become manager of Crystal Palace, but his assistant, Ken Craggs, had stayed on at The Valley and had become the new man in charge. Mullery had also taken Ian Salter, Charlton's reserve team coach, with him to Selhurst Park which had left the vacancy they were advertising for. There had also been some changes at boardroom level, with a young local businessman by the name of Mark Hulyer taking over as chairman from Michael Gliksten, whose family had owned Charlton for some 50 years.

I managed to track Ken Craggs down and gave him a call to say that I was interested in the job. I vaguely knew Ken having met him over the years at different games, and he said that the club were going to hold interviews and invited me down to London to see him and Mark Hulyer. I'm not sure who else was in for the job but I remember thinking it would be great if I got the chance to coach at a club like Charlton. I think they had gained a bit of a reputation as being the club where lots of good, older professionals ended up seeing out their playing days. But the impression I got was that things were changing. They might not have been in the First Division, but it was clear Hulyer had big plans for the club, and he had said that he wanted the team to get promotion. They'd spent some money during the summer and the club itself had a great history and tradition.

At 32, Hulyer was a couple of years younger than me and it was very clear that he seemed to be a young man in a hurry. Whatever people may say about him now and what happened during his time with Charlton, there's no doubt in my mind that the day he walked into The Valley, was the day the club changed forever. The story goes that he walked into the ground one day, less than a year before I actually joined the club, and asked Mullery, "Who's in charge?"

In the absence of the chairman Mike Gliksten, Mullers said that he supposed he was and Hulyer then said that he wanted to give the club £50,000, and in return all he wanted was advertising across the main stand for his company, Marman, for the next five years. Mullery got on the phone to Gliksten to tell him what had happened and not surprisingly the chairman was happy to take the money.

Hulyer was told to come back in a week once the cheque had been cleared, which he duly did and from then on he became a familiar face around the Charlton boardroom and also on the team coach for away trips. During the summer of 1982 Gliksten sold his shares to Marman, and Hulyer, who was the managing director of the company, became the new Charlton chairman. But Gliksten didn't sell The Valley and the whole deal would later go on to have huge repercussions for the club.

I knew it would be a great move for me and I was pleased with the way my interview went. After I left The Valley I made a trip across London to see Dave Bassett, who was managing Wimbledon and had become a good friend after we'd first got to know each other during different coaching courses we had been on. Dave was his usual enthusiastic self and told me he thought it was just the sort of job I needed at that stage in my career. I totally agreed with him and I remember the relief and delight I felt when I was told soon after the interview that I'd got it. The job was a fantastic opportunity for me and a really exciting prospect.

When I turned up for my first day at The Valley I was pulled to one side by Hulyer, who had a quiet word in my ear.

"It's Ken's decision," he told me. "But I'm prepared to go along with it."

Not exactly the kind of ringing endorsement you might want from your new chairman, but it didn't really matter to me. The main thing was that I was the new Charlton reserve team coach and I couldn't wait to get started. I was just happy to be joining a club like Charlton and I was looking forward to getting stuck into the pre-season training programme with a new set of players to work with.

Pre-season is always a busy and important part of any club's preparations for a new campaign. I enjoyed working with my group of players and the club had just joined the Football Combination, which meant the reserves would have regular weekly matches in a league that contained the second teams of several sides who were in the First Division.

One of my most vivid memories of that pre-season was seeing the first team leave The Valley on their way for a tour of Sweden. They were due to fly out from Heathrow, but on their way to the airport and no more than a few hundred yards from the ground, I remember seeing the coach stop at an off-licence while some crates of beer were loaded on! It seems incredible these days to think of that happening because things have changed so much, but football was very different back then and I'm sure the same sort of thing would have been going on at other clubs up and down the country.

While the first team got on with their tour I was busy preparing the reserve squad for the new season and we had several friendly matches lined up before the big kick-off came along. One of them was away at non-league Wealdstone and they had a left-back in their side who looked tremendous. So much so, that the next day I went in and recommended we take another look at the kid because he clearly had the ability to play at a much higher level. I obviously wasn't the only one who thought he had potential because he soon made the switch to the full-time game and went on to have a great career. His name was Stuart Pearce.

The first team got off to a perfect start winning 2-1 at Leicester on the first day of the season, which was just what Ken Craggs must have been looking for. What he wasn't looking for was four defeats in his next four games. One of them was 5-0 against Wolves at Molineux, and I made the trip with the squad. It was a bad defeat but Wolves had a good team at the time and were very strong that season, eventually finishing second in the league to give them promotion to the First Division. I was happy with my own reserve side who were doing okay and I was certainly enjoying the experience of coaching and picking the team.

After those four straight defeats the first team managed to halt the run with a 2-2 draw at Oldham, followed by an important 3-0 home win against Fulham, and it was shortly after this game that news started to break about Mark Hulyer's plan to bring Danish superstar, Allan Simonsen, to the club. As I've mentioned, Hulyer had already signalled his intention to shake things up at The Valley in an attempt to get the club into the First Division, and money had been spent on getting players in, with the likes of Terry Bullivant and Carl Harris joining in the summer. The new chairman had also hit the headlines when it was revealed that the club had tried to sign Kevin Keegan from Southampton. Hulyer, Ken Craggs and Charlton managing director, Richard Collins, had all travelled to Holland during the pre-season period where Southampton were on tour to try and persuade Keegan to join the club. But unfortunately Newcastle were already in the hunt and eventually got their man.

Missing out on Keegan clearly hadn't killed Hulyer's enthusiasm for a big name star, and when the chance to sign Simonsen came along he made it clear he wanted to take it, even if it meant a transfer fee of around £300,000 to Barcelona, which was an enormous amount of money for a club like Charlton. Like Keegan, Allan Simonsen was a former European Footballer of the Year, and there was no way he was going to be a cheap buy. Most people in football were amazed by the story, but Charlton did have a connection with the player, through the club's youth team manager, Ernst Netuka. He was the manager of Simonsen's home town club, Veyle, when he'd joined them as a 12-year-old, and Netuka was also manager of the Danish national side when Simonsen played for them.

The whole saga of whether he would or wouldn't sign went on for more than two weeks before Simonsen was finally unveiled by Hulyer at a press conference in London and confirmed as being a Charlton player. But the drama didn't end there and Simonsen didn't make his first appearance in a Charlton shirt until 9th November 1982, more than three weeks after that press conference. In fact, his first appearance was for my reserve side in a home game against Swansea. He came on as a substitute for the final 40 minutes of the game, but had only been cleared to play just before the kick-off. There was a crowd of about 2,578 at The Valley as opposed to the usual 400 who would have turned up for the fixture, and as well as seeing the club's new star in action, they also saw us win the game 4-1. Four days later Simonsen made his full first team debut for the club when he played in the home game against Middlesbrough, who were managed by Malcolm Allison. It wasn't exactly a dream debut because Charlton lost 3-2, although

Simonsen did get one of the Charlton goals five minutes from time. The Dane was out of the side for the next game at home against Rotherham, because of a hamstring injury, and the poor form continued with the side being beaten 5-1.

I'd taken the reserves to play in a Combination fixture at Upton Park against West Ham, and because it was an early kick-off we were able to get back to The Valley for the final 20 minutes of the game against Rotherham. It was already 4-1 by the time I got there and Ronnie Moore added to the misery three minutes from the end by scoring his third goal of the game. When I saw Ken Craggs after the game he looked terrible. He was distraught and shell-shocked at what had happened and you couldn't help but feel for him. Even though they'd only played 15 league games the signs weren't good and speculation about his future had already started.

Within 48 hours of that result Ken Craggs was no longer the manager of Charlton Athletic. It was brutal really, but very much in keeping with the way things happen in football, probably more so today than back then. A lot of people thought Ken should have been given more of a chance in the job, and the story at the time was that Mark Hulyer had taken Ken out for a meal after the game and said everything was fine, only for Craggsy to be given the boot two days later.

On the Monday morning following the Rotherham game Ken got a message at the training ground asking him to go to The Valley. I think he'd already got a tip from one of the club's directors that he was going to be sacked and had a feeling he wasn't going to be hearing good news when he got back to the ground that day. I remember thinking selfishly that I could be out on my ear as well, despite doing a decent job with the reserves, because that's the way things work and it had happened to me at Plymouth when Malcolm had gone back to Manchester City.

Lennie

At the same time that Ken was heading over to The Valley, Richard Collins was on his way to the training ground to see me. Leighton Phillips was the first team coach and he had a lot of experience as a player and also had a stack of caps as a Welsh international, while Ernst Netuka was also very experienced as a coach. My first thoughts were that if Ken went, one of them would be put in charge of the first team but instead, after going back to The Valley with Richard I was told it was me they wanted to take it on for the next month.

It was supposed to be a short-term appointment to let them have some time to get a new man in. What I could never have known at the time was that I'd end up having the job for the next nine years!

5

ZOOM

It was a fantastic feeling to be put in charge of a club like Charlton, even though I thought at the time it was only going to be for a temporary period. The one thing I was sure of was that I felt up to the task. I was just about coming up to my 35th birthday, so I was still quite young, but I believed I'd had the right grounding to make a go of it because of the time I'd spent at Plymouth and Lincoln and the different jobs I'd done at each club.

I suppose Mark Hulyer and the board must have felt the same and they knew about the fact that I'd fulfilled a similar role with Plymouth before the arrival of Malcolm Allison. To be honest, I also felt that I was ready to take the job on full-time if I got the chance because of the experience I'd gained up to that point. I don't think that would have been the case if Plymouth had given me the job permanently. In fact, it could have been the end of me as a manager if I'd gone into it with so little experience and understanding of what was needed from a manager.

As I prepared the team for my first game in charge as caretaker against Shrewsbury away, I knew that what both me and the club needed were some decent results. I wanted to steady the ship and pick up some points. The team were close to the foot of the table, fifth from bottom of the Second Division, with 17 points from 15 league matches. I got off to a solid enough start in the Shrewsbury game with a goalless draw, unfortunately my chairman decided to take the train to the game and arrived late. I think he was walking up the road as the final whistle blew, so Mark Hulyer wasn't really there to see how the team performed under their new caretaker boss. But he was there for the next game and we managed to get a very important 2-0 win at home against Newcastle. The match was billed as a battle between Simonsen and Keegan. We got lucky that day because Keegan had an injury and wasn't able to play. Simonsen did and scored one of our goals, along with Don McAllister.

From my own point of view it was good to get a win in front of our own fans. They didn't really know too much about me at the time and must have been wondering just what was happening at their club. Don't forget, I was the third manager in a matter of months, and there had already been some changes in the boardroom, with one of the directors, Bill Jenner, leaving and a Nigerian businessman, Chief Francis Arthur Nzeribe, joining the club. Getting the win was nice but it was down to earth with a bump in the next match as we lost 4-1 at Bolton. We bounced straight back from that and beat Barnsley 3-2 at The Valley, so I'd been in charge for four games had two wins, one draw and a defeat. It was good enough for the board and they asked me to stay on as manager until the end of the season.

There had been various names mentioned as possible managers including experienced people like Mike Bailey, Ian Greaves and Malcolm Allison, as well as a couple of older players like John Hollins who was at Arsenal, and West Bromwich Albion's John Wile. It was a great opportunity for me because although the four games had gone relatively well, you really need longer to stamp your mark on a side and it also gave me the chance to start planning and organising the team in the way I wanted to.

I was given the nod just before the start of the busy Christmas period, and we were going to be playing four games in the space of eight days. We drew 1-1 at Crystal Palace, were beaten 3-1 at home by a very good Queens Park Rangers team and then had the prospect of two away games in Yorkshire in just three days. The first was at Rotherham and the second against Sheffield Wednesday at Hillsborough. I decided it would be a good idea to stay in the north rather than come back to London after the first game, but it turned out to be a big mistake.

It's only through experience that you learn about things like this but quite apart from the fact that we lost both matches, there were other problems as well, including not having any real training facilities and losing some of the kit during the course of the trip. It was certainly a learning experience for me and it wasn't all about what happened on the pitch either. During the trip I had a phone call from Derek Hales, who was the club's star striker and is quite rightly seen as a legendary figure at The Valley. He'd picked up an ankle injury in training before the Palace game but was fit enough for the Wednesday match, and although he hadn't travelled north he was supposed to make his own way up there in time to be in the squad for the game at Hillsborough. I'd expected to see him link up with the rest of us at the hotel, but there was no sign of Derek. Then I got the phone call.

"My car won't start mate," Derek told me. "What do you want me to do?"

There I am in Yorkshire in the middle of a hectic Christmas programme, having only been in the job five minutes and suddenly my best striker can't make it to the game because he's stuck in Kent! There really wasn't much I could do and I certainly wasn't going to make a big song and dance about it, so he stayed where he was and we got on with playing what turned out to be a crazy football match.

We were 3-1 up at half-time and ended up losing 5-4. The match also included one of the best own goals you will ever see in your life when Steve Gritt, who also went on to become a Charlton legend, hit a ferocious shot into the top of his own net. I'm sure the goal still gives him nightmares if he's reminded of it, but it wasn't just that mistake that cost us it was playing so poorly in the second half, after playing so well in the first. The result was a real indication of the sort of inconsistency that had caused problems, and it was obviously something I was going to have to try to get to grips with. But that proved to be easier said than done.

Although I'd inherited a squad that had a world class player like Allan Simonsen in its ranks as well as a tremendous goalscorer in the shape of Derek Hales, I soon realised that we were going to be in for a battle. Results had not been great before I took over and after I was given the job we still found it difficult to get wins. In fact, by the time we prepared for the away trip to Burnley in late February, the team had managed only two wins in eight league games. There were a few draws thrown in there as well, but the overall picture both on and off the pitch wasn't good.

Away from the playing side of things I very quickly realised the job I'd taken on would also be heavily influenced by events off the field, something that seemed to be a constant factor throughout the rest of my Charlton career. While I was trying to get things right with the team there was talk that the club were having financial problems and that the reported £324,000 deal that had brought Simonsen to the club had backfired. Rumours suggesting Charlton might have to sell the little Dane began to spread.

Bringing someone like Simonsen to the club had been a huge gamble and Hulyer reportedly thought the club's attendances would rise as a result of having a genuine world superstar for supporters to come and watch, but it never really happened like that. We did have a 16,699 gate for an FA Cup third round match against Ipswich at The Valley, but really attendances certainly weren't high enough to pull in the sort of money Charlton needed for Simonsen, and Hulyer also claimed that sponsorship deals involving the player had fallen through. Everyone knew that Allan was being paid around £1,500-a-week, and this was at a time when the average weekly wage for a player at the club was probably £300 but it didn't stop there, and on the eve of our trip to Burnley a problem with a payment almost saw Simonsen refuse to travel to the game.

We'd finished training on the Friday and were about to leave for the trip to Lancashire, but Simonsen refused to get on the team bus. Apart from his weekly wage, there was also some sort of consultancy or sponsorship deal in place with Hulyer's company in which he was supposed to be paid £17,000 every three months. It was a staggering sum of money at the time and I assume that he had received the first payment in the previous November, but was now due his second which evidently had not gone through. So there we all were, waiting on the bus and he won't get on because he hasn't got his money. Stalemate. In the end Hulyer had to go up the road to a bank in Charlton, withdraw £2,000, put it in a brown bag and give it to him before he would get on the bus. Even after all of that we had to wait for another 15 minutes while Hulyer and Simonsen's representative went into the Charlton boardroom and worked out the exchange rate against the dollar!

He eventually got on the bus and we headed north for what turned out to be an absolute disaster of a game. We lost the match 7-1, Hales and Mark Aizlewood were sent off, goalkeeper Nicky Johns gashed his knee and had to have stitches, while defender Les Berry finished the game limping because of an ankle injury. Just to add to the misery of it all, I got myself booked by the referee after going into his room at the end of the game to ask why my players had got their marching orders. Burnley managed to score five times in a 13 minute spell and if the match had gone on for another five minutes, they would have scored 10, another 10 minutes and it could have been 12. That's the way it was for us on the day, we were absolutely hammered. It certainly wasn't a nice feeling for me to have to deal with and when we got back Richard Collins took me out for an Indian meal in Bromley to try and cheer me up. I think he could see just how fed up I was with what had gone on, and it was actually a nice thing for him to do, because it had been a horrible day all round.

Word got out in the press that Simonsen had originally refused to travel to the Burnley game before finally relenting, although they didn't know the full story, but it soon became obvious that the club could not afford to keep him. It also became clear that there was a real problem concerning Hulyer and the former chairman Mike Gliksten. Hulyer hadn't been able to meet some of the financial terms of the deal they had agreed to when Mark took over the club, and the former chairman was threatening legal action claiming he was owed £420,000. Gliksten had resigned from the board earlier in the season but still owned The Valley, and was due rent under a 30 year lease agreement. It also emerged that he had sold his shares to Hulyer for £1,000 and loaned the club £300,000 to be paid back over a four year period, in quarterly instalments.

Although I was still relatively new to the club, it didn't take a genius to realise there were financial problems looming large on the horizon, but at the same time I couldn't afford to let myself get sucked into what was happening behind the scenes. I had enough to deal with when it came to looking after the team and trying to steer them away from the wrong end of the table. The rumours concerning Simonsen continued, but it was another Charlton player who hit the headlines because of a transfer story in the week following that dreadful result at Burnley, when Paul Elliott left the club to sign for First Division Luton.

Paul was one of the brightest prospects at the club and although he was only 18 years old, he had shown just what a good player he was, and other clubs had not been slow to recognise his potential. One of the last things that Ken Craggs had to deal with after his final game in charge, was a remark made by Emlyn Hughes. He was the Rotherham player-manager at the time and had basically said that Elliott needed to get away from Charlton for the sake of his career. Ken had to deal with that situation on the morning of the day he was sacked, and although plenty of clubs had been keeping tabs on Paul, nothing had really happened until the Luton manager, David Pleat, made his move. Elliott never really knew anything about it until I told him something was happening.

"Something's on," I told him. "Get in your car and meet me at the garage around the corner!"

He didn't know where we were going but turned up anyway. All I told him was that there was a First Division club interested in signing him and that things were moving fast, he followed me in his car as I headed off for the North Circular road and the hotel in Enfield where David was waiting for us. The deal was done pretty quickly and the priority for Charlton was clear – we just needed to get some funds in quickly.

The financial situation was pretty bad and although there were reports that Elliott went for £150,000, the figure was actually less than that, but better than Hulyer had anticipated. Luton still owed us some money on the deal that had taken Paul Walsh to Kenilworth Road during the summer, and the club agreed to take less so long as the money could be paid straight away. With the Elliott deal Luton paid a down payment of nearly £50,000 and the rest of the money was going to be paid after Paul had made a certain number of first team appearances and earned England caps. In all the transfer was worth just under £100,000 and there was a lot of comment about the fact that he'd been allowed to leave the club at a knockdown price, because he'd been talked about as a player who would possibly be worth £500,000. The real truth of the matter was that the club were up against it financially and Hulyer was desperately trying to stave off the problems he was having with Michael Gliksten. To put it bluntly there was now a real chance that the club could be brought to its knees because of all the off-the-field problems.

The writing was also on the wall when it came to the future of Allan Simonsen at the club. After all that had gone on before the Burnley game and with the money troubles that Hulyer clearly had, it was obvious that the Dane's days at Charlton were going to be numbered. The club simply couldn't afford to keep him and it was just a matter of time before he too would become another departure.

In the same week that saw Elliott leave for Luton, Charlton hit the headlines again when it was revealed that both Aston Villa and Leeds were chasing the club for payments. Villa claimed that they were still waiting for two instalments on the £80,000 transfer of Terry Bullivant the previous summer, and Leeds said Charlton had not paid two instalments on the £100,000 transfer of Carl Harris which also took place in the summer. Both clubs issued writs against Hulyer and Charlton as well as reporting us to the Football League.

The one good thing to happen that week was the performance we put in against Chelsea at The Valley. Having conceded seven in our last match at Burnley, we gave ourselves a real lift with a 5-2 win against the West London side. Simonsen was brilliant and scored two of our goals. He showed just what a class act he was and the fans loved it, but two games later he was packing his bags and moving back to Denmark to play for his hometown club, Veyle. Put simply, we just couldn't afford to keep him. When he'd joined, part of the agreement he had was that if Charlton could not guarantee to keep him after June 1983, then he would be free to move, but only to a Danish club. There was no way we could stump up the remainder of the money that we still owed Barcelona, and so the clause kicked in. Simonsen wanted to return to Denmark and bring up his young family in his native country, and on 19th March he played his last game for us in the 1-0 home defeat by Leeds. I suppose if you want to be kind about Simonsen you could say that if you put a great player into an extremely ordinary team, he soon becomes an ordinary player, or you could say he didn't seem as motivated away from home as you would have hoped as a manager. He played 17 games for us scoring nine goals, and technically he was one of the best players I've ever worked with. Looking back now it seems amazing that he ever joined the club in the first place. It was certainly a bold move by Mark Hulyer, but also one that was doomed to fail in a spectacularly short period of time.

With two of the best players in my squad gone I knew a difficult task was going to be even harder as we faced the crucial last couple of months of the season. The stories about our financial plight never stopped, but I was learning that it was all part of the job when it came to being manager of Charlton Athletic. Despite all the problems I was still enjoying being in charge of the team and although it was tough we were managing to keep our heads above the relegation water, that was until we were beaten 2-1 at Fulham and dropped into the bottom three. I always felt we could have a fight on our hands when I took over and by the time the last game of the season at home to Bolton came around, we went into it knowing there was a real chance of us going down into the Third Division.

I knew it would be a really tense affair and in the build-up to the match I tried to do all I could to deflect the pressure that was bound to be on the players. Of course, I was just as worried about our situation as they were, but one of the golden rules in management is to make sure your fears are never transmitted to the team. Malcolm Allison was brilliant at that when I was with him at Plymouth. He would do or say something that made him the subject of attention and the players were able to get on with their jobs without the glare of the media being on them. In recent years, José

Mourinho was superb at doing the same thing when he was at Chelsea.

As we went into the game it was pretty clear what we needed to do. If we won, we stayed up, if we lost, we went down, and if we drew, it depended on what other teams did on the day. Everyone knew it was a massive game, but in my opinion, it turned out to be one of the most significant matches in the history of Charlton Athletic. Not just because of what happened on the day, but because of what was to happen to the club in the years that followed.

Bolton took the lead through Ian Moores just past the hour mark and I knew we were staring down the barrel. The former Manchester City player, Mike Doyle, was playing for Bolton that day and it was his mistake that gave us a lifeline seven minutes later when Derek Hales scored to level. The game turned in the space of 13 minutes, because they collapsed and in the end we ran out 4-1 winners, with another goal from Derek and one each from Steve Gritt, who had come on as a substitute, and Carl Harris. The goals from Derek Hales were crucial and he'd had a fantastic season, scoring 17 goals in what was basically a poor team. During the time he played for me at Charlton we had our ups and downs, but when it mattered he was there for the team, especially at home. I still think the two goals he got in that Bolton game were a huge and very significant contribution from him, and for his exploits over the years with the club, he deserves to be in the Charlton Hall of Fame. In fact, he deserves it for that year alone.

With the season finally over, and with the club's finances still in a precarious position, I had to try and set about planning for the future. About a month earlier Charlton had offered me a two year contract, which I signed. I was going to be earning £20,000 a year, which was probably in keeping with managing the club at that time, but it's amazing to think that some 20-odd years later, most managers in the Premier League would earn that in a week!

The financial problems the club were in certainly didn't go away and that summer it began to look as though things were going from bad to worse. The problems between Mark Hulyer and Michael Gliksten were beginning to turn into a saga, but the club were also hit in July by the news that Leeds were seeking a winding up order. They had got fed up with the fact that they were still owed money on the Carl Harris deal. The Inland Revenue were also after the club for payment of a tax bill prompting talk that Charlton were facing the possibility of going under, not the sort of thing a manager wants to hear as he prepares for the start of a new season, but something that was rapidly becoming par for the course when it came to my job at The Valley.

One of the other stories that surfaced that summer was the proposed bid by Hulyer to buy The Valley from Gliksten. It seemed strange to many people that someone who had failed to find the money for repayments and transfer fees could suddenly come up with the finances to buy the ground. It soon emerged that Mark had actually lined up a backer in the shape of an 80-year-old property millionaire from Kent named Ron Billings. It wasn't the first time his name had been in the press in connection with Charlton, because during the course of the season that had just ended there was a story about Billings buying the ground and turning it into some sort of leisure complex as well. In fact, I met Billings along with Richard Collins on the day after the Burnley debacle, when we went to his place in Kent to talk about his possible plans. In the end he couldn't reach an agreement with Gliksten over the total package and the thing broke down because of that.

When he surfaced once more it looked as though this time it might be different, but again it came to nothing, as did another possibility with a consortium led by the then Rotherham chairman, Anton Johnson, who happened to be a Charlton supporter. Meanwhile, in Leeds High Court the Inland Revenue agreed to an adjournment of the winding up order until early October, so long as a debt of £145,000 was paid which was due in instalments.

This then was the backdrop to the start of my first full season in charge as manager. Hardly the perfect way to prepare for the big kick-off, but when you're in a situation like that there's very little you can actually do about it. I had to concern myself with the things that I could influence, like making sure the squad was properly prepared for the coming season.

Despite all that was going on off the field we started the campaign well, and were unbeaten in our first seven games in the league. We also had the transfer embargo lifted and in September I was able to buy Ronnie Moore for £30,000 from Rotherham, the striker who had done a lot of damage to Charlton in Ken Craggs' last game in charge when they cut us to pieces. There were also some other new faces in the squad, Steve Dowman from Wrexham, Chris Jones who had been released by Crystal Palace, and Peter Mountford from Norwich. By the end of September we were third in the league after a 0-0 draw at Oldham, but we certainly got a rude awakening in the next match as we lost 7-0 at Brighton, and just to make matters worse, the problems off the field began to look extremely ominous.

In what proved to be one of many court hearings over the next few months, Hulyer sorted out the immediate problems from the Inland Revenue, but was then hit by a winding up order made by Michael Gliksten, who claimed he was owed a total of £573,000. Suddenly there were stories about our home game with Manchester City possibly being our last. It was the sort of thing I became used to during the weeks and months that followed, because it was very clear that the finances of the club were in a mess. What ever way it was dressed up the fact was that

Charlton were fighting a real battle off the field, and there was a genuine concern that the club could fold. There seemed to be endless court hearings and adjournments, with stories in the press all the time about how much was owed and how many creditors there were. The situation got more and more acute, and at the centre of it all was Mark Hulyer.

Towards the end of October after a 2-2 home draw with Swansea it was announced that Hulyer was going to step down as chairman and Richard Collins took over, with Mark remaining on the board. It was Richard's task to try and get any possible consortiums interested in investing in the club but it seemed to be a thankless task, and five weeks later he resigned leaving Hulyer back in charge as chairman. The club also decided to sue Michael Gliksten as the court battles raged on. If it hadn't been so serious it might have appeared comical, but the bottom line was that the very existence of Charlton Athletic was at stake, and I still had a football team to look after.

Although managing the side was my main concern, there was no way I could just detach myself from all the problems that were raging off the pitch, and they often had a direct impact on what I was trying to do. We were still playing well in the league and were unbeaten at home as we entered December, but then another little problem reared its ugly head. It was revealed that the club had defaulted on payments they had been due to make to Rotherham with respect to Ronnie Moore's transfer. It ended with Charlton having to go before a Football League hearing, and the club were fined £6,000. It could have been a lot worse because there was the possibility of points being deducted and at the time we had got ourselves into a very respectable sixth in the league. We also had the added problem of having our bank account frozen because of the winding up order, which led to a slightly unusual scenario when it came to getting some of the outstanding money to Rotherham. We couldn't just write out a cheque to them even if we'd wanted to, so instead they were given cash. I'm not sure exactly where it came from but I think we had the money taken from home games, and after one of them I went into the club secretary's office to find cash all over the floor in neatly counted piles. It was then going to be packaged up into blue sacks and quite literally taken up to Rotherham. Different, but then we are talking about Charlton at a time when the old saying, 'expect the unexpected,' was probably the most apt way of describing the day-to-day dealings of the club. I think the whole episode led to a change in the rules when it came to transfers, because after that clubs had to lodge the fee with the league, who then ensured the money was paid to the club receiving the transfer fee.

We lost our unbeaten home record on New Year's Eve getting beaten 2-1 against Huddersfield, but bounced back with a win at Derby by the only goal of the game scored by Steve Dowman. The other good news was that the transfer embargo had been lifted and I wanted to make sure we added a quality striker to the squad. There was nothing unusual in that, because managers are always trying to strengthen their squad. What was unusual, was the player I wanted – Mike Flanagan.

Flan had been at Charlton before, joining in the early 1970's and had only left the club four years earlier in a £700,000 transfer to Crystal Palace. He'd since moved on to Queens Park Rangers and was a proven goalscorer and a classy player. Just the sort of person I wanted to bring into the club. The only problem was he had hit the headlines during his previous time with Charlton for an on the field punch-up he'd had with team-mate Derek Hales in an FA Cup tie at The Valley against Maidstone five years earlier.

Getting the two of them together again made perfect sense from a playing point of view, but I needed to know from the players themselves that there were no problems. Flanagan was going to cost £50,000 and I asked QPR manager Terry Venables whether I could speak to Flan before making any definite bid. I also wanted to talk to Derek Hales to make sure it was going to be alright with him. The two players both confirmed that there was no lasting animosity and I went ahead with the bid. But when news of the signing came out in the press during the week leading up to our FA Cup third round tie at Colchester, Hales publicly threatened to leave the club if we re-signed Flanagan, it wasn't the ideal preparation for the game and I knew I had to take some strong action. Derek was already a legend at Charlton and the fans loved him, but there was no way I was going to have him undermining what I was doing as manager.

I wanted to sign Flanagan because I thought it would be good for the team and knew he would bring something to the club. Hales was the captain of the team and to have him reacting in the way he did was just not on as far as I was concerned, so I told him I was taking away the captaincy, putting him on the transfer list and dropping him from the team for the game at Colchester.

We won the match 1-0 thanks to a lucky own goal from Colchester's Ian Phillips and a couple of days later I had a chat with Hales, letting him know that I was going to go ahead with the Flanagan signing that week. I also explained that I thought he and Flan could give the team a real lift and help us push for possible promotion. Despite all the financial turmoil the club were still in, we were managing to maintain our good form on the pitch and we were sixth in the league. Derek agreed to give it a go and both of them played in our next league game at home to Cambridge. We won 5-2, Hales scored a hat-trick and the two of them worked well together. The week after that game they were pictured together in *The Sun* newspaper sharing a glass of champagne and beaming for the camera, with the story claiming they were now the best of pals!

Lennie

That same week was a good one for me as well, because Mark Hulyer decided that I should have a new contract after the way the team had performed, and he seemed to feel that I'd done a good job in pretty difficult circumstances during the short time I had been in charge. He offered me a four and a half year deal that would take me up to July 1988. It was a long contract and it was nice to have the club showing that sort of faith in me. There was also a nice quote from Mark Hulyer in the press.

He said, "Lennie is arguably one of the top 10 managers in the Football League and has proved his worth since he took over in November 1982. I do not think anybody could have achieved more in such a short space of time. I have no doubt he is one of the most up and coming managers in the game today. I look forward to him realising his full potential with Charlton. Lennie is capable of managing a First Division club and I hope he will do that with Charlton."

The problem was that because of the financial trouble Charlton were in many people seemed to think I might not have a club to manage for too much longer. At the end of January yet another hearing sent a shudder through the club. In the High Court the Inland Revenue asked for a winding up order because they were owed £108,554. Michael Gliksten's Adelong company was also represented and despite having the case adjourned for two weeks, things began to look decidedly bleak. Mark Hulyer got a bit more breathing space when the case was again adjourned for a further two weeks, and it was revealed that the official amount owed to the taxman including VAT was £159,000. I think Mark always knew he had an uphill struggle on his hands, but after that hearing it was clear the hill had turned into a mountain – a mountain of debt.

We went into our league game at Swansea on 25th February 1984 knowing the match might be the last in Charlton's history. They were struggling at the time, but we lost 1-0 to a goal from Colin Pascoe, and two days later the focus was once again on the High Court, with the Inland Revenue seeking to wind up the club. Hulyer put forward a proposal to pay the outstanding income tax debt of £108,000 in three instalments. The money was due by way of cheques from a Swiss company drawn on the London branch of a French bank, and somewhere along the line it all seemed to hinge on a deal involving a shipment of rubber from Bangkok!

The taxman asked for a day to consider the deal, but 24 hours later the proposal was rejected and Judge Mervyn Davies had seen and heard enough, declaring that Charlton as a club were, "hopelessly insolvent," and saying that he had no alternative but to agree to a winding up order. The next day the official receiver had the gates to The Valley locked and bolted, but did allow us to get the playing kit out first, and we basically set up camp in The Valley Social Club just around the corner from the ground.

There's no doubt there was a real air of doom and gloom about the place, and rightly so. The end of Charlton as a football club would have had a huge impact on a lot of people and their lives, not just to the people who worked at The Valley but to the thousands of supporters who had been put through the mill emotionally, and who ultimately could do nothing about what was going on in the courts. To a lesser extent the same is true when a club is relegated, it's not just about the players, there is also a big knock-on effect because a football club is about a lot more than the 11 people who go out and play matches. But although it looked as though things couldn't really get much worse, there was a slight ray of light to emerge in that same week.

Sunley Ltd, who at the time were one of the country's biggest property developers with assets of more than £400 million, were about to try and mount a rescue package. They had been in the background during all of the High Court drama, and the company was based in Beckenham, which was relatively local to Charlton. They also had a man named John Fryer as their managing director, and it just so happened that he was a Charlton supporter and had been since making his first visit to The Valley 57 years earlier. Fryer was actually in partnership with John Sunley, who was the son of the company's founder, Bernard. The other players in the consortium that Fryer was a part of were Mike Norris, a chartered surveyor from Eltham who had a major interest in a London property company and was another Charlton supporter, Richard Collins and Malcolm Stanley who was head of the FADS company that had once sponsored the club when he was a director at The Valley, although he was to later drop out of the picture.

As I have already mentioned, Richard was the man who had tried some weeks earlier to get various consortiums interested in putting together some form of rescue package for the club. From all of that had come the idea of Sunley getting involved, mainly due to Mike Norris and John Fryer getting together. I was aware that a possible rescue bid was being put together, but at the same time I had the job of trying to keep the team focused, and also to publicly put a brave front on things. The Valley Club seemed to become a focal point for everyone, because that was where we gathered to talk about what was happening and to wait on any news. We were in there an awful lot and one thing I vividly remember about those days during that week was that whenever I stepped inside the doors of the social club, there always seemed to be the same record playing in the background. It was called *Zoom* and was sung by *Fat Larry's Band*. To this day if I ever hear that particular record my mind shoots straight back to those dark times when we sat and waited to hear whether there was going to be a Charlton Athletic, or whether a great club was simply going to die and disappear from English football forever.

Although there was fresh hope with Sunley, there was also the problem that they were going to be racing against time to make sure their rescue bid was in place quickly enough to ensure Charlton would continue as a league club. The problem was that the Football League wanted certain financial guarantees from the new consortium before they would give their blessing to the deal. They were also adamant that we had to fulfil our away fixture at Blackburn on the Saturday of that week or be thrown out of the league. On the day after the gates to The Valley were locked and bolted by the official receiver, Mike Hulyer resigned, and the Sunley backed consortium continued their race against time to get everything in place so that the newly named Charlton Athletic Football Club (1984), could make sure the club did not disappear.

The day before we were due to play our game at Blackburn was particularly tense, because so much had to be done in such a short space of time, and all we could do was sit in the social club and wait on phone calls that would hopefully tell us what was happening. There was going to be yet another hearing at the High Court, but before that took place Peter Crystal from Memery Crystal, who were the solicitors acting for Sunley, had to finalise a draft agreement to give to the official receiver. It was mid-afternoon by the time the agreement reached the receiver's offices and they wanted more time to consider the whole thing. This meant having to make a plea to the Football League to allow the Blackburn game to be postponed, something which they had insisted would not be allowed. With the clock ticking away they agreed to a postponement, and in the High Court, Justice Mervyn Davies adjourned the case until the following Monday.

The League's agreement to having the game postponed allowed us to breathe a sigh of relief, but there was no way we could break open the champagne in celebration, because the rescue package had not yet been accepted and we knew we were all going to be put through the mill once more.

We actually had the team bus waiting for us in case we were going to travel to Blackburn, but it was never used. Something else that apparently was never used were the pies Blackburn had ordered in for the game against us, and some time later the club actually got a bill from Rovers asking for £9,000 to pay for them all. They must have been expecting an awful lot of pies to be eaten on the day of that match!

The saga rolled on into the following week, with the Monday High Court hearing being adjourned for 24 hours, but the whole thing was still uncertain on the Tuesday with nothing being finalised, and eventually it was made clear that if a survival package was not sorted out by 5pm on Thursday 8th March, the club would be expelled from the Football League. It meant having to get the High Court agreement to the package, and once again all we could do was sit in The Valley Social Club and wait for news from the court.

I thought the previous Friday had been tense, but it was even worse six days later, because we knew that if we didn't beat that 5pm deadline it would be curtains for the club, and there would be no more second chances. I was getting regular updates on what was happening from various people including reporters with one in particular, Harry Harris, seeming to know exactly what was happening and what the situation was.

When the hearing in the High Court went ahead on that Thursday there was still no guarantee that the Sunley led consortium was going to be successful, and there was still the matter of having Gliksten and Mark Hulyer sort out their legal actions against each other to allow the whole deal to go through. The court had already been in session for 10 minutes when Gliksten and Hulyer agreed to drop their actions and all claims, leaving the way clear for the deal to finally go ahead. Justice Mervyn

Davies eventually accepted the package that had been presented to him, allowing the club to beat the 5pm deadline by the skin of its teeth.

In the end, all that stood between Charlton living to fight another day, or going out of existence was about 30 minutes.

6

HOME AND AWAY

The sense of relief at The Valley Social Club that day was incredible. The whole saga of whether Charlton would survive or not had gone on for so long and with so many different twists and turns, that many people couldn't quite believe it was all over at last.

I suppose that after all that had happened it was typical that the question of whether there would or wouldn't be a rescue package sorted out, went right down to the wire. Under the terms of the deal, Sunley Holdings deposited around £700,000 with the Football League, and preferential creditors got paid in full, while unsecured creditors were to be paid 60p in the pound. It was enough to see the club continue as Charlton Athletic Football Club (1984) Limited, and as well as meaning so much to the supporters, I was also very conscious of the fact that saving the club meant saving the jobs of all the people who were employed at The Valley. Pretty much all the players and staff were in the Social Club that Thursday evening when Peter Crystal came to talk to everyone, outlining just what the takeover meant and how the new consortium hoped the club would progress. I remember thinking he was deeply impressive that evening, and I think everyone in that room was pleased to hear some positive news after all the weeks and months of anxiety.

The first game under the new owners came two days later against Grimsby at The Valley. As you can imagine there was a great atmosphere, and in many ways the result took second place, because everyone at the ground that day realised something much more important had happened less than 48 hours earlier and we were all still celebrating the fact that Charlton still existed. The match should also be remembered for the appearance of a young kid named Robert Lee, who scored on his debut in a 3-3 draw, and went on in future years to rightly be recognised as one of the club's best players. Quite naturally the men at the centre of the consortium takeover, John Fryer, Richard Collins and Michael Norris, were given a great reception by the fans, and it was nice from my point of view that one of the first things they did was to ratify the contract I'd signed when Mark Hulyer was the chairman.

After the Grimsby game there were still 12 matches to go and we were eighth in the league, but we were never quite able to push on from there, as we lost our last five games of the season and eventually limped over the line to finish in 13th place. It was disappointing in many ways not to have made a challenge for promotion, but in all honesty it was amazing that we managed to do so well on the pitch after all the problems off of it. I had been at the club for less than two years, and been manager for a little over 18 months, but I'd managed to pack the sort of experiences into that period that most other people never have to deal with. Looking back now, I'm sure that the whole saga made me a better manager simply because of all the problems I had to deal with on a daily basis, and the conditions I had to manage under.

Quite naturally there were a lot of people ready to point the finger of blame at Mike Hulyer, and there's no doubt that the way he went about running the club eventually saw it almost disappear. But I will always maintain that the day he walked into the offices at Charlton and told Alan Mullery that he wanted to give the club £50,000, was the day the club changed forever.

He might not have known it at the time but his actions, good and bad, were the first steps along the road that eventually saw Charlton return to the top flight of English football and shed the image of being the sort of club where quite a few old professionals could comfortably play out their days. On a personal level I suppose I have a lot to thank Mike Hulyer for. After all, he was the man who gave me the chance to manage a Football League club, and he also backed me by giving me that long contract. He certainly had his faults and they became all too evident at times and were highlighted in the court hearings, but I also believe he went into Charlton with the best of intentions and really wanted to see the club improve. He was young and ambitious with lots of big ideas, and perhaps that was his downfall. The unfortunate thing for the club and its supporters was that the whole scheme was built on sand, and in the end those ideas and plans suffered as a consequence.

I think the prospect of new owners and a new era was exciting for everyone connected with the club at the time, but I also realised that the summer would be a time to take stock, find out exactly what the new people were planning for the club and how they wanted to go about it. One thing I was certain of was the fact that they were not going to go about things in quite the same way as the previous regime.

Having gone through all that I had with the club in a relatively short period of time, I was keen to start moving the team forward. What I didn't want was for everything to stagnate, or for us to miss the chance to go on and build a decent side. I have to say that I wasn't quite sure what was in store for me as we approached the end of the season, even though I had the security of having a four year contract. I didn't feel quite right about my position, mainly due to the fact that I wasn't sure about how the new owners wanted to run Charlton. They'd put an awful lot of money into the club just to make sure it stayed alive, but there's no use being involved in football if you don't have ambition, and I was keen to know exactly what their ambition was and how it would sit with my own plans.

Lennie Lawrence

In the week leading up to the FA Cup final between Everton and Watford that year, Palace sacked Alan Mullery and two days later it was announced that Wimbledon manager, Dave Bassett, was going to take over at Selhurst Park. As I have already mentioned, things happen fast in football, and it wasn't too long before I received an approach from Wimbledon to see whether I would be interested in taking over from Dave. Wimbledon had done brilliantly to rise from being a non-league side, and had just finished the season as Third Division champions meaning that, like Charlton, they would start the new campaign in the Second Division. It was flattering to have another club come after you, and following all the problems we'd had off the field at Charlton, it was tempting to think that maybe a fresh start somewhere else would be good for me at that stage in my managerial career. John Fryer knew that I hadn't been that comfortable in the job towards the closing weeks of the season and on the day of the Cup final he asked me to go over to his house in Shirley, to have a chat with him. It was obvious from the first thing he said to me that it was going to be a clear-the-air meeting.

"You're not happy Lennie, are you?" he asked.

I told him exactly how I felt and let him know that I wanted some sort of picture and plan as to how the club were going to move forward and what they wanted from me. It turned out to be a really good meeting, probably the best I had during all the time John was involved at Charlton, and I left his home with a much better idea of what was going to happen.

He explained that having put so much money into the club just to save it and pay off the creditors, there was no way he and the board were going to start throwing money around. That sort of thing had caused problems in the past, and he felt that his first task was to steady the ship and then try and build gradually towards Charlton mounting a promotion challenge in 12 months time. I didn't really have a problem with that, but my only fear was that if we didn't improve the squad at all we were going to be in for a battle in the season that was coming up. In the end I got the sort of assurances I was looking for and I came away happy in the knowledge that John Fryer was keen to see Charlton gain some success after all the years of struggle, what I had to accept was that it would have to be done in a slower and more methodical way, which once again I had no problem with.

Before any more could come of the Wimbledon job Dave had a remarkable change of mind, saying he had made a mistake, as he left Palace and returned to Plough Lane. He had been away for precisely four days, and his manager's chair at Wimbledon was probably still warm! Dave's decision saw Palace chairman, Ron Noades, take a gamble on 28-year-old former Manchester United and England winger, Steve Coppell, who had just finished his career because of injury. That gamble must have been one of the best of his life, because Steve went on to enjoy great success with Palace, getting them into the First Division by the end of the decade and he rightly became a legend at the club.

The 1984-85 season can probably best be summed up as one of transition for Charlton. There was a lot of movement in the playing ranks, with Derek Hales going to Gillingham in March 1985, after a long and distinguished career in Charlton colours. In all I used 28 players that season and it showed in the way we were never able to produce any great consistency, finally finishing 17th in the league. On a personal note, my marriage to Avril sadly ran its course. For whatever reasons we had gradually grown apart and we split up in December 1984.

The season also saw some additions at boardroom level. Bill Strong, a Greenwich councillor, became a director. This followed a £250,000 sponsorship deal with the council, so it was only right that they should have a voice on the board. Someone else who joined was Derek Ufton who had played football for Charlton and England, as well as being a Kent County cricketer. I later came to realise that he wasn't just a good athlete, but also a really good bloke, and one of the nicest people you could ever wish to meet. Derek was Charlton through and through and knew his football. Someone else who had also played the game was Jimmy Hill, whose views on football were regularly aired during his appearances on *Match of the Day*. Jimmy had also been a manager and a club chairman, so when he was persuaded to join the Charlton board in November 1984, it was looked on as a bit of a coup by many people. Apart from seeing Jimmy on television I never really knew him, but I have to say that soon after joining the club, he began to play a crucial role in helping build the sort of team I was looking for in order to mount a realistic promotion challenge some time down the line.

We started the season quite well and were sixth in September, but then we started to lose our way a bit and by December 1984 we were down to 16th place in the table. I knew we probably had a battle on our hands during the remaining months of the season, but as well as dealing with the week-to-week problems of managing a football club, I also had one eye on trying to plan ahead. I did an awful lot of scouting, looking at players in England and Scotland, where I became something of a regular at midweek matches. I knew I had to start thinking of the future once we got through the season and that meant earmarking the sort of players I wanted to bring into the club.

Shortly after Jimmy Hill joined Charlton he was thrown in at the deep end by being asked to take over as chairman on a temporary basis, because John Fryer had to undergo an operation and was going to be out of action for what turned out to be a number of months. Of course, Jimmy had been a football club chairman before when he was in charge at Coventry City, so he was obviously a safe pair of hands and knew what he was doing. He was also very much a football man and I found that I could get on with him and talk about the game if I needed to. I also told him that I had certain players in mind who I felt could add real quality to the squad, something I believed was essential if we were going to try and make a push for promotion in the next couple of years.

The first of those players was a skilful midfielder who had started his career at West Ham and then moved on to play first for Birmingham and then Aston Villa. He had a very good pedigree and had played most of his football in the First Division, giving him just the sort of background and experience I was looking for. He'd only just turned 27 at the time and I hoped he would not only play a part in helping us battle through the rest of the season, but also in the future of Charlton. Just how big an influence he would have on the club's future I had no way of telling at the time, but in the years to come the signing of Alan Curbishley as a player just before Christmas 1984, was to have a huge impact on the fortunes of Charlton Athletic. Curbs had fallen out with the Villa manager, Graham Turner, and couldn't really get a run in the side. He also fancied a move back south and I think he saw Charlton as a club that would allow him to do that and at the same time offer the chance to play regular first team football, even if it was for a Second Division side struggling to keep their heads above water.

We sorted the deal with him at the Royal Lancaster Hotel in West London, with Jimmy, me and Arnie Warren, who was my chief scout at the time, but also much more than that. Arnie had been in the game for a long time and was the sort of wise older head I needed alongside me after becoming a manager. Although he was the chief scout at the time, he later became general manager, and was a great help to me. In many ways he would have made a terrific director of football these days, and when he joined me at Charlton I remember saying to him, "Arnie, see the mistakes coming, and stop me making them," which was exactly what he did on many occasions. I will always be grateful to him for that and for all the other invaluable assistance he gave me during the time we worked together and over the years since then.

The reason we used the hotel was because we didn't really fancy the idea of Curbs seeing The Valley before he signed in case it put him off! Let's face it, he'd just come from a club that had recently won the European Cup and just a few days before he came to meet us, Curbs had been in a Villa side that played a home game against Liverpool in front of 40,000 people.

Jimmy agreed with me that Curbs would be a great addition, and he sanctioned the transfer, which was going to cost the club £38,000. We signed Alan and the next day he had to come to The Valley for his medical. I could tell from his face that he wasn't too impressed with what he saw because the ground was pretty dilapidated compared to what he'd been used to. In fact, he's since said that the best thing about that particular day were the roast beef sandwiches I sent out for from the pub around the corner.

The good thing was that I'd got the first piece in the jigsaw, and towards the end of the season I managed to get another when we paid Celtic £40,000 for left-back Mark Reid. I'd seen him playing for their reserves on one of my many trips north of the border and could see he was a really good defender. Once again he had a good pedigree and experience, playing first team football for Celtic as well as winning league and cup medals with them. I was delighted to get him and over the years that followed, Mark showed just what a good piece of business it was, because he was one of the most consistent players we had and a great professional.

We were beaten 5-1 by Manchester City at Maine Road on the last day of the season, but managed to stay up, finishing 17th. Soon after the season ended I was able to make another crucial purchase when we signed big John Pearson, a striker from Sheffield Wednesday, for £100,000. It was a lot of money but John Fryer was being as good as his word and I knew the club were going to back me that summer as I tried to put together a side that would see us competing at the top end of the table in the coming season, instead of at the bottom of the division.

Once a season is over it's always nice to be able to relax a little, even if it is usually only for a matter of weeks. After signing John I decided to take up an offer from Crown Paints who sponsored Liverpool, to watch the Merseysiders in the European Cup final against Juventus in Brussels. It should have been a wonderful experience, but instead it turned out to be a nightmare. What happened at the Heysel Stadium that day was nothing short of a tragedy when 38 people lost their lives and around 400 were injured after trouble between the two sets of supporters. The game was delayed and eventually finished 1-0 to the Italians, but like a lot of other people I left long before the final whistle, and will always remember the sense of terrible sadness I felt when the full reality of what had happened sank in.

The summer of 1985 was a busy one for me and for the club. Having started to put those jigsaw pieces together when I bought Alan Curbishley, and then carried on the building programme with Mark Reid and John Pearson joining the club, I wanted to make sure I began the new campaign with the sort of squad I felt would give us a realistic chance of having a go at promotion. Backed by John Fryer and the board I brought in five more players; midfielders Jimmy Loveridge from Swansea on a free and George Shipley from Lincoln for £15,000; central defenders John Pender from Wolves who cost £35,000 and Steve Thompson from Lincoln for £25,000 as well as right-back John Humphrey from Wolves for £60,000. So apart from Curbs I'd also recruited seven other new players and we kicked off the new season with a 2-1 home win against Burnley. I had made sure the mixture of the squad was right and was determined that it shouldn't all be players who came from London, once I'd got the people in that I wanted, I was quietly confident that I had a squad capable of making a challenge.

We made a good start and were unbeaten in our first four league games, with everything to look forward to as I prepared the team for the visit of local rivals, Crystal Palace, early in September.

From my previous experiences with the club I should have known that just when I thought things were going to plan, something would come along to completely change the picture, and sure enough that happened on the night before the game when I got a phone call from the Charlton secretary, Graham Hortop. He said he'd called to prepare me for what was going to happen the next day. Put simply, the club were going to announce their intention to leave The Valley and would instead be playing their 'home' games at Palace's Selhurst Park ground. To say it was a bit of a bombshell would be an understatement. I knew the club had been having problems with the ground, because the Greater London Council had deemed the huge East Terrace to be unsafe and had stopped fans using it. As if that wasn't bad enough Michael Gliksten, who still owned the ground and rented it to the club, decided that he wanted to use two acres behind the West Stand and there was speculation that he might want to develop the land. All of this had apparently combined to force the hand of the board and more particularly, John Fryer, who decided the best course of action for the club would be to move out completely and share with Palace.

As you can imagine, it wasn't the sort of thing I had planned for as I concentrated on getting the team right, and I knew the fans would not only be really upset at leaving The Valley, but also understandably angry. Just to top it all off, we were going to have Palace as our landlords. Hardly the sort of atmosphere I needed going into the game with them, but one that I knew I had to deal with in the best way I could. I told all the players that I wanted them at the ground early for the match, and when they'd all arrived on that Saturday morning, I let them know exactly what was going to be happening that day. In an absolute PR disaster as far as I was concerned, the fans were handed leaflets which were distributed before the match, telling them that their club was going to be moving to share with their bitter rivals – brilliant! Just to rub salt into the wounds the leaflet with the heading, 'Message To Our Supporters,' then went on to tell the fans how to get to Selhurst by train and by bus. You couldn't really make that sort of thing up, but that's how curt the whole thing was. Understandably, the fans were not happy with the new arrangement, and there were some very angry supporters at the game. At least we managed to win 3-1, but there was a terrible atmosphere that day, with Charlton supporters knowing our next home game against Stoke in two weeks time would be the club's last at The Valley.

We lost our unbeaten record in the next match when we went to Oldham and were beaten 2-1. Naturally I wanted us to bounce straight back with a win against Stoke but I was conscious of the fact that there was going to be a lot of emotion on the day as the fans said goodbye to their beloved Valley. There were half-time demonstrations with fans staging a sit-in on the centre circle, and at the end of the game supporters started tearing up bits of turf to take away as souvenirs. We won the match 2-0 with goals from two of the team's young players, Mark Stuart and Robert Lee, but it was terrible for the supporters and many of them vowed never to make the seven mile trip to Selhurst Park. It was a very sad day all round and I'm sure there were a lot of people who thought the club would never be able to return to their home again.

But something else happened after that match against Stoke on 21st September 1985, because I believe it was the day Charlton Athletic became more than just a football club, it became a cause.

7

HOUDINI

The move was clearly difficult to take for the supporters and it soon became apparent that an awful lot of them were determined to somehow get the club back to The Valley at some stage. What was also obvious was the fact that, certainly in the short term, we were going to have to get used to playing our home games at Selhurst.

Palace's ground may have only been seven miles away but it was a terrible journey for the fans and took absolutely ages. As for the players, I have to say that it was probably not such an emotional wrench for most of the team, simply because about eight of them were relatively new to Charlton, and the ones who had come in the summer hadn't really had a chance to get used to The Valley. They understood how the fans felt, but at the same time I think that as a team, the main priority for everyone was to try and make sure we maintained our focus, which was to get promotion at the end of the season.

After the win against Stoke we lost 3-1 at Wimbledon and then drew 1-1 at Bramall Lane against Sheffield United, so by the time the first game at our new 'home' arrived against Sunderland at Selhurst, we were in need of a win. It was a funny sort of atmosphere for the match and I suppose I wasn't sure exactly how the whole thing would go, what I did know was that we needed the points and thankfully we got them winning 2-1 with goals from a Mark Reid penalty and another from Mark Stuart seven minutes from time.

I have to admit it was all a bit strange as we tried to get used to Selhurst being our new home. The club had portakabins put up to use for offices, but we weren't allowed to train on the pitch before a game and I felt that we needed to have a working base that we could truly call home. Fortunately a businessman called Frank Allen, who happened to be one of my best friends, had an interest in a sports ground at New Eltham. It used to be owned by the Unilever company, but they had sold it to Frank and two of his mates. The place was not only used as a sports ground, it also had a club house and dressing rooms and at the time was being used by Millwall as a training ground. I spoke to him about it and he agreed to let us begin using it instead of Millwall. It allowed us to have a base and it became very important to the team because we were able to use it throughout the week and that was where all of our work was done. The other good thing was that as well as having the pitches for the team to train on I also had a little office there. The funny thing was that it was still being used for functions at the weekends, and quite often we'd return from an away trip on the team bus and the place would be buzzing with people having a party, and a disco blaring away in the background!

Despite the move it soon became apparent that we were going to be in with a realistic chance of challenging for promotion. We were always there or thereabouts in the league and when it came to the final push, I genuinely believed we could make it, but I also thought I needed to get someone in who might give us that little bit of extra firepower when the going got tough during the final couple of months of the season.

I was at Manchester City looking at a midfielder who played for Newcastle, called Alan Davies. I wanted to take him on loan, which was what I eventually did, but during the course of the match a player who really took my eye was the City's Scottish striker, Jim Melrose.

The City manager, Billy McNeill, was sitting just behind me in the stands so I asked him if there was any chance of him letting Melrose go and he said yes. It was as simple as that. I'd gone to look at one player and saw another that I really felt would do a job for us. I was right because Jim went on to play a huge role for us during the remaining games of the season and also throughout the time he stayed at the club. Sometimes things like that can happen for a manager. It's an almost instant decision that comes off and pays dividends.

Melrose made his debut at The Den against Millwall, scoring in a 2-2 draw. It was another vital point for us and by the time we played Fulham on a Tuesday night in late April at Selhurst Park, we were within touching distance of realising the dream and taking the club back into the top flight of English football after an absence of 29 years. We won 2-0 with one goal from John Pearson and an own goal from Fulham's John Marshall. We were all but there and the fans that night started to celebrate when they ran on the pitch afterwards, but we still couldn't afford to get carried away because I knew we had the chance to make it mathematically certain with our game at Carlisle four days later. Obviously it was a big game for us, but in many ways it was an even bigger one for them, because they needed to win to have a realistic chance of staying in the division.

We took around 2,000 Charlton supporters with us for the match and it looked as though we might disappoint them when Wes Saunders scored twice for them in the first half, but we got back in it five minutes before the break thanks to an own goal from Jim Tolmie, and then two more from Mark Stuart and Mark Aizlewood in the last 20 minutes of the game gave us the win we all wanted. We really could start to celebrate, and that's just what we did. I was even chaired around the pitch at the end of the game by some of the Charlton fans who had made the trip north, and so was John Fryer. It was a tremendous feeling for all of us and it was also unique. We'd managed to win promotion to the top flight of English football while playing most of our home games on another club's ground.

Lennie Lawrence

It had been another amazing season for me as manager of the club. Since the day I first took over from Ken Craggs there hadn't really been a dull moment. Not all of them were good, but winning promotion and doing it in the circumstances we did, seemed to make up for all the bad times. The club had come through an awful lot and so had I, in what was a relatively short period of time. As Derek Ufton said to me, "Whatever happens in the future, you'll be prepared because of what's happened here."

He was right and there's no doubt that I really came of age as a manager during those first few years at Charlton. You always know that the nature of the job means you are going to have to deal with at least one problem every day of your working life. The problems can be small or they can be big, and at Charlton during those years and the ones that followed I had to deal with some pretty big problems, but the truth is that I loved it. I suppose it might be the way I'm built, but I honestly felt the job suited me and I suited the job. Getting to the top league in the English game had been a struggle and a tremendous achievement but I knew as we celebrated after our last game of the season – a goalless home draw with fellow promotion winners Wimbledon – that both the club and myself were going to be facing another massive challenge when the new season started as we tried to compete with the big boys.

I think a lot of people couldn't quite believe we'd be playing our football in the First Division, but the fact still remained that a lot of supporters were very unhappy at us playing home games at Selhurst and were desperate for a return to The Valley. As manager I was aware of the depth of feeling there was, but at the same time my main priority was with the football team and I knew I just couldn't afford to let myself get bogged down in all the politics which were constantly swirling around the club.

I knew that life in the First Division was going to be tough and after the euphoria of promotion had died down it was my job to try and prepare a squad for the rigours of what was to come. As usual I realised there wasn't exactly going to be much money for me to play with when it came to trying to strengthen the squad, but that was always going to be a fact of life and I just had to get on with it. I suppose it was quite natural for people to believe we were likely to be lambs to the slaughter, but although it was going to be difficult I knew my main job was to try and ensure we survived.

I was able to make a key signing in late July when I persuaded Sheffield Wednesday defender, Peter Shirtliff, to sign for us. The fee was £125,000 and he ended up being one of the top 10 signings of my whole managerial career. He proved to be a great defender during his time at Charlton and immediately became a major player in the side. Shortly after getting Shirtliff, I signed goalkeeper Bob Bolder from Sunderland for £20,000. At the time it seemed a pretty unremarkable piece of transfer business, but Bob was another player who went on to play a huge role in the club's history during his time with them and once again, I would say that he was also one of the top 10 signings of my career.

We started the season with a 1-1 draw at Selhurst against Sheffield Wednesday, thanks to a Robert Lee effort, but only 8,501 people watched us play our first 'home' game back in the top flight, and it was obvious there were still many fans unwilling to turn up even though we were now playing First Division opponents. We lost three and won one of our next four games, but the victory was certainly a memorable one because it came against Manchester United at Old Trafford, when we beat them with the only goal of the game scored by Mark Stuart. On the team bus after the game I sat next to John Fryer. He'd ploughed an awful lot of money in since taking over the club and I was delighted that he'd got to witness the victory against one of the giants of English football.

"There you go Mr Chairman," I said. "You've seen us get our first win in this division and you were able to watch it from a seat in the director's box at Old Trafford."

"F*****g expensive seat!" he replied referring to how much he'd spent on the club since becoming chairman.

I still wanted to strengthen the team and knew that the midfield area looked a little weak. Alan Curbishley wasn't available at the time because he'd had an operation, and I didn't want the team to struggle in that department.

Just before we were due to play Liverpool away in September, I managed to make a double signing that I felt gave us the sort of midfield strengthening we needed. First I went to Grimsby and signed Andy Peake. I drove all the way to Grimsby and was quoted a fee of £80,000, but I simply told them I could only pay £75,000 and the deal was done with me driving back to Andy's house before heading to London with him for a medical.

In the same week I travelled up to Nottingham with Arnie Warren to sign Colin Walsh from Forest. I'd been trying to tie the whole thing up for some time, but their manager, Brian Clough, sometimes wasn't the easiest person to get hold of on the phone. On one occasion I tried to speak to him only to be told that I had no chance because it was a Thursday and he always took his dog for a walk on a Thursday afternoon. When we eventually did turn up at the Forest ground everything was shut up at the main entrance and we ended up having to knock on a door. Cloughie actually opened it but clearly wasn't too impressed to see Arnie and me standing there.

"Oh it's you," he said in a matter-of-fact way, and then walked off, leaving us to do the deal with Forest's secretary. He clearly wasn't interested in getting involved in the sale of one of his players, but some months later

I saw a different side to him when we were both interested in a player called Paul Wilkinson. Paul was with Everton at the time and I was looking to bring in a striker to help us in the last few months of the season. One evening the phone rang and I heard the familiar tones of Brian Clough on the other end, although at first I actually thought it might be one of my mates doing an impression of him! It quickly became clear I was talking to the real Cloughie and unlike the encounter with him when we went to sign Colin Walsh, this time he was more than happy to talk before getting to the reason for the call.

"Lennie I understand we're both interested in signing the same player," he said.

I told him that from what I'd heard Wilkinson had set his sights a bit higher than Charlton and wanted a bigger club with more chance of winning things, so it didn't look as though we were really in the running. He was obviously pleased to hear this and a few weeks later got his man when Wilkinson signed for Forest. It was interesting to see how different Cloughie could be and I certainly experienced two very different aspects to the character of a man who was quite rightly regarded as one of the greatest managers the game has seen.

Walsh cost us £125,000 and once again it turned out to be money well spent. In fact, it was a real bargain because he did a great job for me and for Charlton during his time with the club, becoming a real favourite with the fans who enjoyed having such a class performer to watch. Getting Walsh and Peake certainly strengthened the squad, but I knew we were going to be up against it. We did have a very good month when we remained unbeaten in October and we got ourselves up to 12th place in the league table, but then had a disastrous November losing all five games in the league and it was clear even at that stage that we were in for a relegation battle.

When you're in a situation like that it's important to have the right sort of people in your side and I knew I had a good set of lads in the squad who would go out and give everything. I also wanted to freshen things up a bit as we entered the second half of the season, and there was a bit of a turnaround on the playing front, with John Pearson and Mark Aizlewood both going to Leeds.

In came midfielder Ralph Milne from Dundee United and defender Paul Miller from Tottenham, a player who was to have a massive influence on what happened that season. Miller was exactly the sort of character you needed in a battle, because it was the sort of situation in which he excelled. When I signed him I knew what sort of player he was, but it was only towards the end of the season that I realised just how important he was to us.

Ironically, although we were having a tough time of it in the league, we managed to do well in the Full Members Cup and after beating Birmingham, Bradford, Everton and Norwich, found ourselves in the final at Wembley against Blackburn Rovers at the end of March. Obviously my main concern was making sure we stayed in the First Division, and I didn't want our progress in the competition to be a distraction, but once we'd reached the final it was good for everyone involved to see the club in a Wembley final for the first time in 40 years.

I've already mentioned that John Fryer had put an awful lot of money into the club since becoming involved with Charlton, and he clearly wanted to make sure there was no repeat of the financial problems we'd had in the recent past. He was rightly careful about any money we spent, but there was one instance leading up to the final that staggered me. Like any team who reach a Wembley final we wanted everyone to look smart in a set of suits that we were going to have specially made for the big day, but when it came to getting the money for them Fryer would only cough up for 11 plus two more for the substitutes! It meant that the rest of the squad wouldn't have the same suits, and we would have looked ridiculous. In the end I had to beg, borrow and steal the money in order to get extra suits for everyone involved.

One person who I decided wasn't going to be involved in the final was Alan Curbishley, and he didn't take being dropped too kindly. He came storming into my office at the training ground on the day I announced the team and the substitutes and a few tasty words were exchanged between us, but the simple fact was that I was the manager and I'd made my decision. Curbs had struggled after having an operation and he hadn't really played too many games. On the day of the final we all had our picture taken on the pitch after the players had walked around Wembley to get the feel of the place. Curbs was in the picture with the rest of the squad, but that was pretty much the last time we saw him that day, because after the team got changed and prepared to go out for the match, he turned the other way and walked out of the stadium. He's told me since that by the time Blackburn's Colin Hendry scored the only goal of the game in the 85th minute, he was back at his house in Essex having taken the tube home. There were 43,789 fans there and it was a great day out for our supporters, even though we ended up losing a game we should have won, but there was no time to dwell on what had happened because there were still nine league games left, and we were fourth from bottom of the league.

A few days before the final I'd managed to make another signing when we got Garth Crooks in from West Bromwich Albion, he was an experienced striker, had been at Spurs with Miller and knew what it was like to play in big games with a lot of pressure. With two games of the season to play, pressure began to be something we all became very familiar with.

We'd just lost at home to Luton and were in the bottom three having won only once in our previous six matches. I must admit that when Mick Harford scored for Luton with only four minutes on the clock remaining I thought that was it. We had to play Newcastle away and QPR at home knowing that to have any realistic chance we would have to win the games.

We went to Newcastle and came away with a 3-0 win, which was an absolutely fantastic result for us. Miller, Crooks and a young striker called Carl Leaburn scored the goals. Miller was a massive influence not just on the pitch, but also off of it and unbeknown to me he'd taken it upon himself to talk to the players the night before the game. He told them he hadn't come to the club to get relegated and really stirred them up. It certainly had the right effect and he led by example the next day, just as he would do later in his Charlton career when the chips were down. We also managed to pull off a win in our last game against Rangers with a penalty from Colin Walsh a minute before the break and another goal from Garth Crooks 10 minutes after the break, but Leroy Rosenior scored for them in the 69th minute and from then on we looked petrified except, that is, for Paul Miller. He was kicking everything that moved. The result meant we finished fourth from bottom and would have to go into the end of season play-offs.

The play-off format has become an accepted part of the game now, but back then the way it operated was different and, in my opinion, it was better. These days the team that finishes fourth from bottom is safe. Three teams at the bottom of the table are relegated automatically and are replaced by the two top sides from the division below, while the teams who have finished third, fourth, fifth and sixth in that division battle it out for the other promotion place. Back in 1987 the team finishing fourth from bottom in the First Division had to play a two-leg game against the side who finished fifth in the Second Division, while the third and fourth placed teams in that division did the same, the winners of those encounters then went on to play in a two-leg final to decide who would get the prize of a place in the First Division for the next season.

We had to face Ipswich, playing games away and then at home in the space of four days, while Leeds did the same against Oldham. The first game was played at Portman Road on the Thursday following our win against QPR. We drew 0-0, which was a good result but we could have done even better, because after just 11 minutes Colin Walsh was tripped by Ian Atkins in the box and the referee awarded a penalty which Walshie took. Unfortunately Paul Cooper in the Ipswich goal did really well to push it against a post to make a great save.

We went one better in the second leg winning 2-1 with two first half goals in the space of three minutes from Jim Melrose, and although they came back and scored through Steve McCall with five minutes of the game to go, I never really felt worried and was always convinced we would go through to the play-off final, where we would be playing Leeds after they beat Oldham on the away goals rule having drawn on aggregate 2-2.

We didn't have too long to prepare for the Leeds game because it came along six days after the Ipswich match. Just to add a bit of spice to the occasion both Mark Aizlewood and John Pearson were in the Leeds team that ran out at Selhurst Park for what proved to be a tight game with Jim Melrose getting the only goal of the game three minutes from time.

He popped up with some vital goals for us throughout that season and when it was all over he'd scored 17 in all competitions, which shows you just how important he was during that first season after promotion.

Two days later we were off to Elland Road for the second leg played in what was an electric atmosphere. Leeds can be an intimidating place to go to and the crowd seemed to be baying for our blood as soon as we arrived at the ground. The team bus was surrounded by their fans and I had a real go at the police inspector who was supposed to be in charge of security, because quite simply there wasn't any. We had to run the gauntlet as we made our way to the dressing rooms, but the team dealt with the whole situation well, in front of a crowd of 31,395, most of whom were desperate for Leeds to beat us. We lost the game 1-0 with their goal coming from Brendan Ormsby after 52 minutes, but the good thing was that we never caved in after conceding and with the aggregate score level, we had to meet them again four days later on a Friday night at Birmingham's St Andrews ground for a one-off match that would decide who was going to take the prize of a place in the First Division for the next season.

There were 18,000 people in the ground that night and the noise was deafening. The Charlton supporters were outnumbered by about 20 to one, and some people thought Leeds might be too much for us, but I felt we'd been the better team over the two legs, although both games had been incredibly close. At the end of the 90 minutes it was still 0-0 and we went into extra-time. What happened in the 30 minutes that followed was life changing for a lot of people involved that night, and for the two clubs.

After nine minutes of the extra-time period John Sheridan scored for them and the place erupted. I knew we were staring down a barrel just as we had been in that game with Bolton four years earlier. Peter Shirtliff had been a tremendous buy for us and had performed brilliantly throughout the season. He was a great defender with a cool head on his shoulders, and someone you always felt you could rely on. Despite all of those qualities I never thought of him as the man who could score vital goals for us, but he certainly proved me wrong that night. First he scored our equaliser when he knocked the ball in after Mark Stuart had laid it back to him, and then with three minutes of time remaining on the clock a well worked free kick involving Colin Walsh, Steve Gritt and Andy Peake saw the ball delivered into the box for Shirty to come storming in to power home a header. It was a killer goal and totally knocked the stuffing out of Leeds and their supporters, because there was so little time left for them to do anything about the situation.

The goal owed a lot to my coach Brian Eastick, who had gone over the move with the players the day before the game. It was actually a move we worked on quite a lot during the early part of the season, but then dropped it, only for Brian to resurrect it to dramatic effect in our very last game of the season. I was delighted for him, because he was a good coach and seeing something come off like that in such an important game must have been fantastic for him. I was also delighted for the players and the fans. It was an amazing night for all of us, but emotionally very draining. After the match I did the usual press conference but although I was standing there answering questions, my head was somewhere else. I was shattered and still trying to take in all that had happened.

Once I'd spoken to the press I went to see Leeds' manager, Billy Bremner, who was an absolutely cracking bloke. He had been a great player and part of the famous Leeds team of the 1970's when Don Revie was manager. I knew how much the defeat must have hurt him, but he was really dignified about the whole thing. In the months that followed there were consequences for both Billy and some of the players, with Howard Wilkinson taking over as manager at Elland Road heralding a new era that would eventually see them win the First Division championship five years later.

We had survived against all the odds and I could start planning for another season in the top flight. Some people began to call me Houdini saying I'd managed to mastermind an escape act that nobody thought was possible. Little did I know at the time that it was an act we would all need to perform once again less than 12 months later.

8

SURVIVORS

What happens in the summer at a football club can often have an effect on the season that follows. Players can be bought and sold, while a manager may be sacked and a new one appointed. These sort of things are commonplace in the game, but what happened in the boardroom at Charlton in the summer of 1987, was to have a profound impact on the direction the club took over the next few years.

In June John Fryer stood down as chairman and a new figure in the shape of Roger Alwen became a director. Richard Collins again took over as the club's chairman, but it was Alwen and Mike Norris who very quickly became the guiding force. Jimmy Hill had left the club a couple of months earlier to become chairman of Fulham, and although he was given a bit of stick in some local quarters for the role he played at Charlton, I have to say that I had a lot of time for him. What a lot of people either chose to forget, or didn't realise, was that he was the man who had sanctioned the purchase of the players I'd brought to the club during the period he was acting chairman. Those were the same players who formed the backbone of the side which got us promotion. He was always very supportive and backed my judgement in the transfer market, which is something a manager always needs from a chairman if he is going to function effectively and build the kind of side he wants.

Having escaped by the skin of our teeth in the season that had just finished, nobody wanted a repeat performance. I may have picked up the Houdini tag, but it wasn't something I intended to be a permanent fixture on my managerial CV. Once again I knew we had to strengthen the side. We'd survived with a ridiculously small squad for a First Division club, and the playing depth was paper thin. I needed numbers and I needed quality players with proven ability. I knew I couldn't go out and compete with the really big clubs, because Charlton simply didn't have the resources to do that, so it was a case of being careful and picking the right sort of player.

Someone who I thought fitted the bill was midfielder Steve Mackenzie, he had been signed as a 17-year-old from Palace by Malcolm Allison when he was at Manchester City for £250,000 which was then a record for a teenager. He'd moved on to WBA for £650,000 two years later, and I managed to get him for £200,000, which I thought was good business. He was still only 25 and was just the sort of quality midfield player I was looking for, particularly as I knew I was going to lose another one.

Alan Curbishley had struggled with injury and fitness in the season that had just finished, it was also difficult for him because when he was available I already had a pretty settled group in the middle of the park and that meant he had to take a back seat. Brighton had shown an interest in him during the season and had been relegated to the Third Division. Their manager, Barry Lloyd came calling again that summer and I told Curbs that I thought it might be a good move for him, because I certainly couldn't guarantee him regular first team football. I liked Curbs, not just because of his quality as a player, but I'd also noticed during his time at the club that he was very single-minded and never afraid to say what he thought. He would have a go at the other players if he believed things weren't right and I think they respected him for it. Just before he left I pulled him to one side and said that if I was still around at Charlton in a few years time I would get him back to the club as a coach. I'm sure he thought I was just saying it as a parting gesture, but I meant it.

I also knew that getting our pre-season preparations right was going to be important. None of us had really had much of a break because the play-offs went on for so long. They were physically and emotionally draining for everyone involved, but I had to make sure the players were going to be in the best possible shape for the new season and decided to take them to the Royal Marine training camp in Lympstone for our first week back in training. It was physically demanding and also a good team building exercise which I thought went well.

Meanwhile Mike Norris and Roger Alwen's influence began to be felt, when the two of them bought our training ground from Frank Allen and his partners, paying £250,000 for it and then spending a further £250,000 doing it up and providing the sort of facilities that were the envy of quite a few much bigger clubs in the First Division. The training ground had always been important to us because, as I mentioned earlier, it became our base once we had to leave The Valley. Now the club actually owned the facility and it began to function solely as a training ground for Charlton Athletic.

Despite what I thought had been a good pre-season period we didn't exactly start the new campaign in great fashion. We lost 2-1 at home to Nottingham Forest on the opening day of the season and then went five league games without a win. We finally broke our duck with a home win against Luton when Crooksie scored the only goal of the game, but it was hardly the start of brighter things to come and despite paying £350,000 to Port Vale for striker Andy Jones, we never really got going. The results didn't pick up and we were bottom of the league with two wins from 17 games by the time reigning champions Everton arrived at Selhurst Park in early December. We got a goalless draw from the match, but there were only 7,208 people at the game, which I found staggering. We were playing the champions of England and I thought we could have attracted more interest from the fans, but perhaps I was being a bit naïve. There was still a lot of bad feeling from Charlton supporters about the fact that we had moved away from The Valley and were playing at Crystal Palace's ground. Some had stuck to their vow of never watching the team again as long as they were playing at Selhurst. Those fans got some good news in March 1988 when it was announced that the club intended to quit Selhurst by the start of the 1989-90 season, and that Roger Alwen and Mike Norris had paid around £2.5 million for The Valley, but it was unclear what would happen to the site and where exactly Charlton would move to once they left Selhurst.

Meanwhile, our form had improved enough to give us a fighting chance of not only avoiding relegation, but also the prospect of more nail-biting games in the play-offs. In order to do that, we had to go to Chelsea on the last day of the season and avoid defeat, while they needed to win, because although we were a precarious 17th in the table, they were one place below us.

I knew the game at Stamford Bridge would be a tight and tense affair, but what I hadn't been prepared for was the fact that it turned into something akin to World War Three! I can honestly say that I've never seen anything like it from that day to this. The referee, Darryl Reeves, had to call his two linesmen over to ask for some help in spotting incidents off the ball. It was a battlefield rather than a football field that day.

Paul Miller was absolutely magnificent and sometimes it looked as though he was playing them on his own. I had my ups and downs with him during his time at the club, but I have to say that in the game against Chelsea he showed some astonishing qualities. I feared the worst when Chelsea went ahead with a penalty from Gordon Durie after 16 minutes for an incident that was clearly out of the box, but the team were tremendous and they got back on level terms 20 minutes after the break, when Miller looped the ball over Kevin Hitchcock in their goal. Carl Leaburn got flattened by Steve Wicks in one incident and had to be restrained from going after the Chelsea man when he came round. It was that sort of game, but at the end of it we had got the point we needed. It meant we'd guaranteed another year in the First Division and avoided the dreaded play-offs, it also meant some of those Houdini headlines were dusted off and used again. There was no messing about from us after the game either. Our team bus had been parked about a mile away from the ground after it had dropped us off, and once the game was over we didn't hang around. Instead, we used a couple of minibuses that brought some of the Charlton staff to the game, and all the players loaded themselves on to them before being driven to the team coach. I knew before the game that it was going to be a bit of a World War Three situation in footballing terms because it meant so much to each club, so my thinking was that we were just going to focus on the job in hand and then win, lose or draw, we were out of there as soon as possible.

The season might have been over but I had another big day to take care of in May when I married Lyn and there was a partnership of a different kind announced that same summer when it emerged that Roger Alwen and Mike Norris had become joint owners of the club. It meant that Sunley's were no longer involved, but it was clear the two men had a very definite idea about what they wanted to do, and that was move the club back to Greenwich and possibly The Valley.

Having flirted with relegation for the past two seasons nobody wanted to have to do the same again, but there really wasn't much money around for me to try and bring in new people. The good thing was that we had some decent young players coming through from the ranks, and I'd also bought a young striker named Paul Williams from non-league Woodford

Town a couple of years earlier. He was 23 and I'd given him his debut in the previous season, but I decided he might be able to do a job for us as we started the 1988-89 campaign. He took to it all like a duck to water and began to score some important goals, although we still found it difficult to put the ball in the back of the net. What we did have was a pretty decent defence which I was able to reinforce with the arrivals of Colin Pates from Chelsea and Tommy Caton from Oxford. The hero of Stamford Bridge, Paul Miller, went in the opposite direction when I sold him to Watford after he was sent off for a spitting incident against Newcastle in September. We weren't exactly high-flyers in the First Division and spent most of the time near the bottom end of the table, but we kept our heads above the relegation water and there was a huge boost for the supporters with two months of the season remaining.

In March 1989 Roger Alwen took over as chairman of the club with Mike Norris becoming the vice chairman. In the same month in a meeting at Woolwich Town Hall Roger announced that the club intended to go back to The Valley. It was just the sort of news the fans wanted to hear, suddenly after all the years at Selhurst there was a chance to return to their true home, but the old stadium had been left to rot since we'd moved out, leaving the place overgrown with weeds and in need of a lot of cleaning up.

The club had the idea of asking fans to go along to The Valley on a Sunday morning early in April 1989 to start clearing the site, in an effort to once more make it resemble a football ground. Thousands of people turned up that day and it was a truly remarkable sight. I remember turning up and it was a very damp and misty morning. When I got out of my car I heard a very strange sound. It reminded me of a scene from the film, *Papillon,* where the prisoners are chained as they trudge along to be shipped off to Devil's Island, because I could hear a kind of clinking noise. It was echoing around the place and turned out to be all the supporters clearing weeds and trying to generally clean the place up. It was truly remarkable to see so many people out there on the terraces and pitch, all genuinely delighted to be involved in helping get their club back to the ground they loved so much. If anyone was in any doubt about the emotional attachment the place had for so many supporters, they should have taken a look at those people that day.

On the pitch the team did their bit and with a game to go we managed to ensure that we'd be playing First Division football again the following season as we finished in 14th place. It was a stunning achievement in many ways, but it was still obvious that it was never going to get any easier and trying to sustain our status for a fourth year was always going to be an uphill task.

Although it was my job to concentrate on getting the team right to play in the First Division, there was no way I could ever ignore the fact that the move back to The Valley was always very much in the background, no matter what happened on the pitch. The club held an open day at the training round in August and without doubt the thing that produced the most interest was the scale model of the proposed new Valley. I think it gave everyone a lift at the start of that season, but by December there was a very different mood at the club.

On the pitch there had been changes with Peter Shirtliff moving back to Sheffield Wednesday for £500,000 and another defender, Joe McLaughlin, coming to us from Chelsea for a club record £600,000. But things didn't exactly go to plan and after a decent enough start we began to lurch alarmingly towards the relegation zone. By the end of the year we were bottom of the league and the club's plans for a new stadium were running into trouble with the council, when the planning application was blocked. The second half of the season proved to be no better for us and on 17th

April 1990, our great First Division adventure came to an end with a 2-1 home defeat against Wimbledon. Even before Wimbledon finally killed off our chances of staying up, I remember thinking that we were gone. In the end we were relegated by a country mile and finished the season second from bottom with our South London neighbours, Millwall, below us in the table.

We played our last game in the division on 5th May at Old Trafford, losing 1-0 to Manchester United in front of more than 35,000 people. Two days earlier a remarkable thing had happened in the borough of Greenwich when the local council elections had taken place. Fed up with the council's attitude towards a proposed move back to The Valley, a group of fans decided to form The Valley Party and contested 60 of the 62 seats in the elections. The only seats they didn't fight belonged to the two councillors who had voted for a return to The Valley.

The newly formed party produced a tremendous poster campaign which tried to show the history of the club and its importance to the area. When the votes were counted The Valley Party had polled 14,839, which was quite amazing and showed once again the depth of feeling that existed amongst the supporters. I knew the proposed move back to The Valley would have a huge knock-on effect for me, because you didn't have to be a financial genius to realise that the whole project needed to be funded and that, in turn, meant I would be expected to sell some of our best players. Once the season was over we went on a tour to Australia and I remember looking at certain players and thinking that it would probably be the last time I'd see them in a Charlton shirt. Sure enough there were some departures that summer. The biggest loss as far as I was concerned was John Humphrey who went to Palace for £450,000 in total, £70,000 of which was part of a maintenance bill for Selhurst! John was one of the best professionals I've ever worked with and a fantastic bloke to have around. In many ways his going signalled the start of a trend that continued during the summer and throughout the season that followed.

There was also a departure on the coaching front at the end of August when Mike Flanagan left the club. I had brought Flan back almost three years earlier when Brian Eastick left to become manager of Newport. Mike had done well for me with the first team, but at the start of the new season after we'd lost our first game 2-1 at Selhurst to Swindon, he went on a local radio station the next evening and was openly critical of the way I wanted the team to play. I'd opted for a 4-3-3 formation which had worked well in pre-season, but we had looked well off the pace in the Swindon game. Once I heard about what Flan had said I felt I had to take some action. There's no point in having a first team coach who clearly didn't agree with what the manager of the club was doing, so I called him in and let him know exactly how I felt. The end result was that he was first suspended and then left the club.

Although Alan Curbishley had been a bit sceptical about my parting comments to him three years earlier when he'd joined Brighton, I was actually as good as my word and during the summer of 1990 I brought him back to Charlton as a player-coach with responsibility for looking after the reserves. When Flan left I did the coaching myself for a while, but then decided it would be the right thing to move Curbs up from looking after the reserves, to coach the first team. At the same time Steve Gritt, who was still playing, took on the coaching role with the reserves. Curbs was still fit enough and good enough to play, not just for the reserves but also the first team, and by the end of the season he'd chalked up 21 games.

Our form wasn't great at the start of the season and we had to wait until the end of September for our first win in the league. We then went four more games in the league without a win and it was around this time that there started to be speculation about me and my position as Charlton manager. It actually reached a point after one home game where Roger Alwen felt it necessary to go up to the press room after the match to clarify the situation. The fact was that although I felt I was doing my best in difficult circumstances, the results just weren't coming and it just added to the pressure. On top of all of this there were the almost daily rumblings about the club's proposed return to The Valley, which had hit another snag when the revised plans they wanted to submit were held up by a dispute involving the NALGO union at the council offices.

Thankfully things started to pick up and from having hit rock bottom with a 2-1 home defeat against Watford in October, we managed to climb a little by the end of the year and although we knew by that time that it was going to be a struggle right the way through to the end of the season, I at least felt that we could avoid the prospect of a second successive relegation, which would have proved disastrous. Nevertheless, I have to say it was a really tough season for me. There were some good young kids coming through and I'd managed to make some decent buys in the shape of Stuart Balmer from Celtic and Simon Webster from Sheffield United, but it can best be summed up as a season of struggle and consolidation on the playing field. Another player who came to the club early in the New Year was defender Alan Kernaghan from Middlesbrough, who proved to be a very good player and did a great job for us during a loan spell. By the time Easter came along we were safe from any possibility of relegation and off the field there was more good news, when the club's revised proposals for The Valley finally got the go-ahead. It meant the board and everyone else could start planning for an emotional return at the start of the following season, and our final first team game at Selhurst was a 1-1 draw against West Ham on 4th May 1991. We had been away from The Valley for more than five and a half years. An awful lot had happened during that time and surviving in the First Division in the way we did, on such small resources, is an achievement I am proud of to this day, but the club needed its own home and The Valley was always the place everyone wanted to go back to.

We ended the season with a 2-0 defeat at Plymouth leaving us in 16th place in the table. As I walked towards the dressing rooms after the match it was hard for me to take in just what had gone on in my career since that first day at Home Park where it had all begun when Mike Kelly appointed me as a coach. It had all started for me at Plymouth, but I had no way of knowing on that day in May that after nine amazing years Home Park was going to be the place where I had my last match in charge of Charlton Athletic.

9

DIFFERENT WORLD

Apart from getting away on holiday for a few days after the season had ended I spent the early part of the summer in 1991 trying to prepare Charlton for a new campaign, which at the time, looked as though it would be starting with the team playing back at The Valley.

I was doing the usual sort of things any manager tends to do in the summer. Plan pre-season, decide on possible targets in the transfer market and start to release those players you think you can do without. Once again it was obvious there wasn't going to be too much money around, but I didn't want another season of struggle. I knew we probably weren't going to be in a position to challenge for promotion, but I did want to start building a squad that might be in with a realistic chance in the not too distant future.

With the move back to The Valley I realised that I might be called on once again to make playing sacrifices in order to help fund the project. At the same time the board agreed that the purchase of someone like Alan Kernaghan would make sense if I was going to start building a decent squad again, and I certainly saw it as an investment, not only in the team, but also because I felt his value as a player was only going to increase. I was given the go-ahead to talk with Middlesbrough to see if some sort of deal could be worked out, and started negotiations with them in June, but by the end of the month their manager, Colin Todd, had left the club and I thought his departure might throw a spanner in the works. A new manager coming in might want to take stock and may not fancy getting rid of Kernaghan.

It was at this point that I began to talk to Middlesbrough's chief executive, Keith Lamb, because he was handling any possible deal with Kernaghan. The fee that was being talked about was £300,000, which was quite big money, and Barnsley were also in for him as well. But I was always confident that Alan would come south and join us, and those 10 good reasons to do so that I mentioned at the start of the book, seemed to be swaying his decision in our favour. As I have already mentioned, I had no idea that Middlesbrough might be looking at me as the person they wanted to replace Toddy, so when that call from Keith Lamb came, I was completely unprepared for what he was asking me.

The upshot of all of this was that early in July I found myself sitting in a private room at the Royal Lancaster Hotel in London talking to Keith and the Middlesbrough chairman, Colin Henderson. By the end of the day we'd talked the whole thing over and tentatively thrashed out a deal. I drove the two of them to Heathrow airport and knew as I dropped them off that the whole thing was beginning to move with pace and I needed to speak to Roger Alwen about what was going on. It was all very hush-hush, and during the time all of this was going on I went to a 25th wedding anniversary party for Frank Allen and his wife Jackie. It was really awkward for me, because I couldn't even tell Frank what was going on.

Keith and Colin were keen for me to go up and meet them early the following week to tie things up, and in my own mind I knew that it was the right time for me to move on. I had been at Charlton for nine years, but with all that had happened, it felt more like 15 or 20! In life and in football I have always made decisions using my instinct. On this occasion my instinct was telling me it was the right time to go, even though I knew that leaving the club after being with them for so long was going to be a wrench.

I thought I had done my time with Charlton and it was just too good

My first job in professional football. Here I am with Plymouth (front row, fourth from left) along with manager Malcolm Allison (front row, fourth from right).

LINCOLN CITY F.C. 1980/81

Back row
G.HOBSON, D.BELL, S.WARD, G.CREANE, T.CUNNINGHAM, J.SAUNDERS, S.THOMPSON, S.HIBBERD, I.TRAVIS, G.SHIPLEY.
Middle row
L.LAWRENCE(Coach), P.TURNER, S.NAYLOR, M.HARFORD, N.KEELEY, C.BOULTON, W.BIGGINS,
T.PEAKE, K.FOX, C.RAMSAY, B.LOXLEY(Physiotherapist).
Seated row
D.BURROWS, T.THOMPSON, G.T.BLADES(Director), H.C. SILLS(Director), J.H.SORBY(Company Secretary).
J.SHERIDAN(Ass.Manager) C.V.MURPHY(Manager), H.W.DOVE(Chairman), D.W.HOULSTON(Director)
A.C.DAVEY(Vice Chairman) D. HUGHES, D.CARR.
Front row
A.McLAUCHLAN, D.GILBERT.

A team picture during my time at Lincoln where I got all the rough edges knocked off me thanks to manager Colin Murphy. That's me, first on the left in the second row.

Letting my feelings be known from the Charlton dug-out in 1986.

My first ever signing, Tyrone James, during the time I was Plymouth caretaker manager.

Opposite and Above: Accepting a Manager of the Month award during my Charlton days.

Anxious looks from a packed dug-out at Carlisle as Charlton go for promotion.

Celebrating with my Charlton team after beating Fulham when promotion was within touching distance.

The hat might not be flattering, but I couldn't be happier after gaining promotion with Charlton.

Football may be my game but I also love cricket and here I am in action during a charity event involving the Master of Dulwich College's XI against the Lord's Taverners in 1986.

Dave Bassett and me posing for the camera after both Wimbledon and Charlton went up to the top flight.

Early days at Charlton after taking over as manager.

A dinner with some of my Charlton colleagues (left) and another 'do' (right) this time while I was at Plymouth with Malcolm Allison.

Fans clearing weeds at The Valley as they tried to get the old stadium ready for an eventual homecoming.

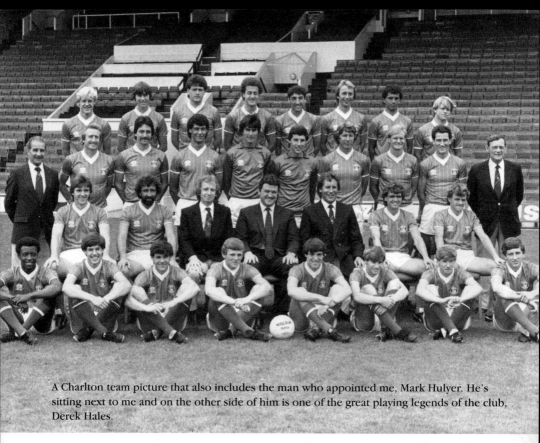

A Charlton team picture that also includes the man who appointed me, Mark Hulyer. He's sitting next to me and on the other side of him is one of the great playing legends of the club, Derek Hales.

Middlesbrough celebrating after our promotion.

Looking on from the touchline when I was **ma**nager of Middlesbrough.

Pointing the way at Grimsby.

A great moment for Cardiff after gaining promotion through the play-offs, here I am on the pitch after the match with Sam Hammam.

Partners. Paul and me at Bristol Rovers.

Looking on after the Johnstone's Paint Trophy defeat by Doncaster, but better times were to follow a few months later with promotion.

Having a quiet word with Bryan Robson before a pre-season friendly when he was in charge at WBA.

Congratulating Trolls.

All smiles after getting promotion with Rovers.

Happy to be a Rover. A picture taken on the day I became their director of football.

an opportunity to turn down. It had been a fantastic adventure but it was time to move on, what I will for ever regret was the eventual manner of my departure. I went along to Roger's house to let him know the situation and he gave his formal consent for me to talk to them about the job. They wanted me to go up and speak with them on Tuesday 9th July, the same day that I had already agreed to take part in a photo-shoot which involved me sticking my head through a cardboard cut-out of a player, to try and encourage season ticket sales at Charlton.

After doing all the publicity for the season tickets I flew up to Teeside and met with the Middlesbrough people at the Crathorne Hall Hotel. As well as Colin and Keith I also met a fresh faced director of the club named Steve Gibson, who was to go on and have a huge influence on Middlesbrough a few years later. By the end of the evening the deal was done and everything agreed. It was as simple as that. They were absolutely paranoid about the appointment getting out, and had arranged a press conference for the following day, which meant they wanted me to stay in the north east and be paraded in front of the media the next day. It's easy to say it now, but what I should have done was have further conversations with them and then gone back to Charlton before everything came out into the open, but Middlesbrough were determined to get everything done there and then. Roger clearly thought I'd just gone up to talk to them and suddenly on the Wednesday it was announced that I was the new Middlesbrough manager. Happily the unfortunate end to my time at Charlton has not soured my relationship with Roger, and we remain friends to this day, but at the time I think it left a bitter taste not only for him, but for a lot of people connected with Charlton. Some fans saw it as an act of treachery and there was talk at the time of the club demanding compensation. It wasn't the best way for me to leave, but I had made my decision and the prospect of moving on was an exciting one for me.

Ironically I'd got the offer from Middlesbrough at the end of possibly my most indifferent season in charge at Charlton. Sometimes things like that happen in football management, and sometimes you have to even get the sack before moving on to a better job. I had made the decision to go because I felt it was the right move for me at the right time. If I'm honest I suppose I was probably finding the whole job at Charlton a bit wearing. There was, quite rightly, a pre-occupation with returning to The Valley and I had gone along with selling some very good players in order to help fund the move. I knew there was a distinct possibility that I would have to sell again and I think I felt that the prospect of going to a club who would give me a fresh start and hand over a bit of cash to build a team with was very appealing at that time.

That doesn't mean to say that I left Charlton on a whim. It may have happened very quickly but I gave the situation a lot of thought before agreeing to become Middlesbrough manager. Most people seemed to think I would always be at Charlton, simply because I had been there a long time and gone through so much with the club, but the chance to manage Middlesbrough was just too good to say no to. It was probably the swiftness of the whole episode that surprised many people, and that was to include my wife, Lyn. Shortly before Middlesbrough became interested in me I'd taken her to the airport so that she could go for a week's break with some of her friends. When I saw her off I was the manager of Charlton Athletic, but when her mother went to pick her up I was the new manager of Middlesbrough! As I've already said, things happen quickly in football.

I'd be lying if I said there was no element of sadness about leaving Charlton. It had been a wonderful experience for me and I had met and worked with some fantastic people. Not just players and coaches, but all of the office staff. We were like a big family and it was a special time. The spirit and loyalty of the fans had been amazing. Yes I would have liked to have had bigger crowds at Selhurst during our time there, but I could fully understand the depth of feeling shown by some supporters when it came to having to leave The Valley. The sense of achievement we all felt at beating the winding up order, getting promotion and then managing to stay in the First Division was immense, and rightly so. We had all been involved in a unique experience and those memories will always be a part of me, but it was time for both me and the club to move on. When I first became manager of Charlton I told the board that I not only wanted to build a team, I also wanted to build a club, and I feel I did that.

Of course, I had a lot of help along the way, from many different people and someone who was fantastic during my time with him was Arnie Warren who, when I left, had the title of general manager. I think Arnie had a lot to do with making sure things went smoothly after my departure when the board made their decision about who should take over from me. Like a lot of other people, Alan Curbishley had been caught cold by the news that I was going to leave Charlton. In fact, he was still on holiday when he was told. He spoke to me when he got back and asked if I wanted him to come with me, but I thought it was all a bit too soon for him and so he stayed. Shortly after I departed for the north east the board surprised a lot of people by opting for Curbs and Steve Gritt in joint player-manager role, and in doing so they began a chain of events that would see the club go from strength to strength.

The two of them did a fantastic job together for the next four years and then in the summer of 1995, Charlton decided to split the partnership giving Alan the job on his own. Everyone in football knows the story of just how well it went for him as he led the club to promotion twice, and established it as a recognised Premier League outfit before leaving them in the top flight in the summer of 2006 having done 15 years at the helm.

A fantastic achievement, but I know that like me he has been saddened in recent years to see the club experience two relegations after all those years of stability. Between the two of us we saw the club through 24 years, and I doubt if that will ever happen again.

Charlton did eventually get back to The Valley, although not by the start of the 1991-92 season as they had hoped. Instead, there were yet more delays in the move, with the club having to ground share, this time with West Ham United at Upton Park, before the historic return to their own home on 5th December 1992 when Colin Walsh scored the only goal of the game against Portsmouth, more than seven years after Charlton had first left The Valley.

Not surprisingly, one of the first things Curbs and Gritty wanted to do when they took over was carry on where I had left off with the Kernaghan deal, but although I had been given the go-ahead to press on with the transfer, they were told that the money wasn't available any more. First lesson of management, one day the money's there, the next day it's gone!

Meanwhile, having given Kernaghan 10 good reasons why he should join Charlton, I was busily giving him another 10 good reasons to stay at Middlesbrough. Happily it worked and I knew he would go on to become an important part of my plans for the club that season.

They say it's good to hit the floor running when it comes to a new job, but in my case I didn't just run, I was forced into a sprint. Pre-season was already underway and I knew I couldn't afford to hang around when it came to getting a squad together with the right people in place. To say it turned out to be a frantic pre-season period would be an understatement. There were all sorts of things going on, because as well as the regular work on the training pitch and in friendly matches I was also trying to get a cohesive team and pattern of play to evolve.

On my first full day in the job I made a point of seeing all the players individually for a chat. I had seen Middlesbrough play near the end of the previous season when they lost 2-0 in an away game with the eventual Second Division champions, Oldham. It was a game Boro should have won and I'd gone there to keep tabs on Kernaghan who had gone back to the club after his loan spell with Charlton. Although I had no idea at the time, the match also meant I got to see at first hand some of the players I would later inherit. Middlesbrough went on to lose in the play-offs to Notts County, and for whatever reason, quite a few of the squad were either out of contract or seemed to be unsettled at the club. When I saw each of them to have a chat the bottom line in the conversation was simple, did they want to stay at the club, or did they want to go? About half of them wanted to go and then there were others who had fallen out with the previous manager, Colin Todd, and maybe saw it as a chance to make a fresh start at the club. They were a close, tightly knit group who had been through a lot together. People like Colin Cooper, Kevin Poole, Simon Coleman, Ian Baird, Trevor Putney and John Wark, all eventually left, while I brought in striker Paul Wilkinson and midfielder Willie Falconer from Watford and full-back Curtis Fleming from Irish side, St Patrick's Athletic.

I came across a familiar face soon after arriving at the club when I bumped into a guy called John Pickering. I'd known him at Lincoln when we were both on the coaching staff and we hadn't always seen eye to eye at the time. When he turned a corner at the ground and saw my face I doubt that he was too pleased, because he probably thought I would bomb him out. In fact, what happened was that he ended up being my assistant, and appointing him was one of the best things I ever did. I had originally tried to get Peter Eustace to join me. I'd had him working as a coach at Charlton during my time there and when I went to Middlesbrough he was working with Frank Clark at Leyton Orient. I offered him the assistant manager's job, but Frank then moved upstairs with Orient to become managing director and Peter took over as manager. John Pickering and I were like chalk and cheese, but the chemistry worked. He was deeply respected by all the players and was highly organised. He was an absolute diamond of a man and a tremendous help to me throughout my time at the club. Having the right person working alongside you in football management is so important.

As part of the pre-season we played a friendly match against St Patrick's in Ireland on a terrible pitch, and my most vivid memory from the trip is of the last day as we waited for the team bus that would take us to the airport. We were all sitting on our cases outside the hotel when this ancient looking coach rattled along the street and shuddered to a halt in front of us. The driver looked as though he was still drunk from the night before, and we had to load our gear onto the bus as best we could. The thing could hardly move as we squashed inside it, and it looked like a scene from the 1960's American TV comedy, *The Beverly Hillbillies*, as we set off down the road going at about 10 miles an hour!

The first game of the season was a home match against Millwall, who were managed by former Boro boss, Bruce Rioch, and they also had Colin Cooper in their side. I have to admit that later on in his Millwall career, when he was switched from left-back to centre-back, I regretted letting him go. Having said that, he was determined to leave when I first arrived and there seemed no point in making things awkward. We beat Millwall with the only goal of the game from Robbie Mustoe, and then lost our next two away at Derby and Ipswich. I tweaked the way we were playing a little and things started to pick up, and we hit a winning streak of six matches leaving us top of the table. Getting Paul Wilkinson in from Watford gave the team more definition because he was able to lead the line so well. It was one of the reasons I had tried to get him to come to Charlton a few years earlier, when he was at Everton and ended up going to Forest. I had a good bunch of committed players in the squad with some very decent youngsters coming through like midfielder, Jamie Pollock, who was a local lad and only 17. But it was really a wafer thin squad and I knew I would need reinforcements in order to see us through the season.

I was also always very conscious of trying to balance the books in the transfer market. In November defender Tony Mowbray left the club in a £1 million deal with Celtic. Tony had been at Middlesbrough a long time and was the captain. He just felt that he needed a change of clubs at the age of 27 and once that was made clear, all I could do was get the best deal for Middlesbrough. Celtic only wanted to pay £800,000 for him, but I managed to get it up to £1 million, which was good business. Later in the month I spent £750,000 on a striker when we got Andy Payton from Hull and then I went back to Charlton and paid them £150,000 for Andy Peake. We'd lost Tony but I'd managed to get two more players in and still showed a profit from the deal with Celtic.

Once Mowbray had gone I handed the team captaincy to Alan Kernaghan and made Mark Proctor the club captain. I have to be honest and say that I didn't exactly have the smoothest of relationships with Proctor, or with another established player, Bernie Slaven, but that sometimes happens in management. You can't expect to be all things to all players and there are always going to be a few feathers ruffled along the way. The truth was that the team was working hard for me and for each other. They were getting their reward with some very decent results, and we stayed in the top two until December. We also did well in the Rumbelows Cup, beating Bournemouth, Barnsley, Manchester City and Peterborough to reach the semi-final stage where we met Manchester United over two legs in March.

We drew the first leg at home 0-0 in front of 25,527, which was our biggest home gate for four years, and then lost 2-1 at Old Trafford. Lee Sharpe gave them a first-half lead, but then Bernie Slaven equalised for us and the game went to extra-time.

About 12 minutes into the extra period it looked as though Falconer was going to score for us, until Peter Schmeichel stuck out a hand that seemed to stretch for about 10 feet and made a superb save. United finally won the game with a goal from Ryan Giggs, but we had given the best team in the country a real run for their money. We also got through to the fifth round of the FA Cup but blew it against Portsmouth and lost 4-2 in front of our own fans after doing the hard bit by drawing 1-1 at their place.

However, the real aim for everyone was to try and win promotion, but as the last part of the season approached we found ourselves in seventh spot in the division and there weren't too many people who were backing us to go up automatically in one of the top two spots with just six games to go. We started the sequence of matches well enough beating both Oxford and Plymouth 2-1 in front of our own fans, but then suffered a real sickener when former Boro player, Peter Davenport, scored the only goal of the game for Sunderland at Roker Park. We had three matches left and they all came within the space of a week. We had home wins against Bristol Rovers, 2-1, and Grimsby, 2-0, before travelling to Molineux for our final game of the season against Wolves. The scenario was simple. Win and we were up. Any other result meant the outcome was out of our hands.

The drama of the day started early when we got a phone call at our hotel to say the police had found some gun cartridges in the middle of the pitch and they were a bit concerned. There was also a fire in one of the stands that day, but the game went ahead. Just to add to the tension of the occasion, I was forced into having to give a debut in goal to Ian

Lennie

Ironside, because our regular keeper, Stephen Pears, who had been terrific all season, was injured. I'd let Ian know early on that he would be needed for the game and tried to give him as much protection from the media glare as I could in what I knew would be a real pressure situation. On the day he never let me down and neither did the rest of the team. It was goalless at the break and then they went in front with a goal from Andy Mutch, and as if that wasn't bad enough we then had Nicky Mohan sent off when he tried to break up a scuffle involving other players. Happily, Jon Gittens, who had come on loan from Southampton, equalised for us and then we got a dramatic winner through Paul Wilkinson, even though it was something of a fluke. He knocked it in with the side of his head from a cross by Jamie Pollock. That was it. We were up and the celebrations started.

I was chaired around the ground on the shoulders of supporters, much as I had been after the promotion season I'd had with Charlton, but my overall emotion as everyone went wild around me, was one of relief. I was relieved not only to have got promotion, but to have avoided the prospect of the play-offs. We had played an awful lot of games that season, more than 60 in fact, and I honestly don't think we would have had the legs to carry us through the play-offs. They would have been too much for us.

What happened that day was a very different experience compared to what had happened 12 months earlier at Plymouth. It seemed like a different world, and after all the celebrations had died down I began to focus on the more practical matter of how we were going to prepare for life as a team in the first year of the Premiership.

10

ALL CHANGE

The scenes as we looked down from our open topped bus were tremendous. The team had been given a civic reception and it was something we could all enjoy and appreciate after coming through right at the end to clinch promotion.

There was a lot of satisfaction in knowing that I'd managed to get the team up in my first season in charge, but when I had time to sit and contemplate what had happened and what was likely to lie in store for us, I came to the conclusion that we weren't really ready for the Premiership. To put it in a nutshell, we had done it all too quickly. I'm not even sure the board thought that I'd be able to get the team promoted in my first season, but that's what happened and I knew it was now my job to do the best I could against the top sides in the country.

I'd been there before with Charlton and even though Middlesbrough were probably better off and better equipped, there was still a nagging feeling that it might be a real struggle to maintain our place in the newly formed league. For a start we had a pretty small squad and although there was some quality within it, I wasn't going to have the sort of money that would allow me to go out and buy the established proven performers at that level who would have helped us. What I wasn't aware of at the time, but have since learned, was that my 'failure' on three counts in the transfer market that season, began to sew doubts in the mind of Steve Gibson, who would later go on to have a very big say in the direction the club was going to take.

Even before the end of the previous season Stuart Ripley had been to see me to say that whether we got promotion or not, he felt it was the right time for him to move on from the club. It was something I didn't want to get caught up in at the time, because we were desperately trying to make sure we went up, but I told him to wait until the summer and see if he still felt the same way. Despite gaining promotion Stuart did feel the same way and nothing that I could say was going to stop him from wanting to leave. In the end he went to Blackburn in a £1.3 million deal and I bought Tommy Wright from Leicester City for £650,000. I also had a couple of other transfer targets in my mind; one was midfielder Gavin Peacock who was at Newcastle and the other was a player I knew really well, Robert Lee, from my old club.

Trying to sign Gavin had turned into a bit of a saga for me, because I'd wanted him to come to Charlton when he was a 15-year-old, but it never happened. Instead he'd gone on to play for QPR, Gillingham and Bournemouth showing what a quality player he was, and had been a big success in the north east with Newcastle. One of the last things I did as Charlton manager was to bring his father, Keith, back to the club as part of the scouting staff. He was a legend at The Valley who had played more than 500 league games for Charlton during the course of a long and distinguished career.

I spoke to Keith about the possibility of his son joining us and I actually talked to both of them. At the time it seemed as though Gavin wanted to move back south and I thought that I would have to face the fact that he would find his way to one of the top London clubs. But in the end Newcastle manager, Kevin Keegan, persuaded him to stay at the club and Gavin didn't see joining us as a step up, even though we were going to be playing in a higher division than Newcastle. He stayed on and ended up being a real force in their team as they won the First

Division championship.

Not getting Robert to sign for us is something I still regret to this day. It was my fault and a bad mistake on my part. He oozed class and at 26, was coming into the prime of his playing career. I had seen what he could do as a youngster and of course, gave him his league debut in that famous 3-3 drawn game at The Valley against Grimsby, when he'd scored one of the goals in the first match after the new John Fryer consortium had stepped in and saved the club. He would have been a major asset for us after getting promotion, but instead of going to Charlton and blowing them out of the water with an offer neither they, nor Robert could refuse, I was too slow and a bit complacent. Perhaps it was the fact that I'd been used to trying to get players as cheaply as possible, or that I knew Charlton needed the money because although they were still using Upton Park as their home, they were scheduled to finally return to The Valley by the end of the year. The team had done really well under Curbs and Gritty, going close to getting into the play-offs during their first season in charge, and Robert had been a big part of that. I knew they wouldn't want to lose him but I also realised, probably better than anyone that the club wanted to bring in some much needed cash for their biggest playing asset.

I started off with an offer of £250,000 which Curbs and Gritty said no to. I thought it was worth a try just to test the water, but once it was rejected I put in another bid of £400,000. I later found out that Curbs tried to get West Ham manager Billy Bonds interested in buying Robert. Once Alan and Steve knew that they were definitely going to lose Robert, it was their job to try and bring in as much cash for the player as they could. Robert was a West Ham fan but Billy wasn't interested in going any higher than £500,000. Then Newcastle became interested in Robert and the whole thing began to rumble on and become a bit of a saga. I had to wait while Colin Henderson got the bank to make funds available for me to bid £700,000. I spoke to Robert about a possible switch to us and a move to the north east. The impression I got was that he thought it was too far for him to move, but not too long after that he'd signed for Kevin Keegan – Newcastle is even further away from London! To be fair to Robert, I think Keegan was a boyhood hero of his and he also went on to have a fabulous career with Newcastle and play for England, so he made a good career decision but it was a blow to have missed out on someone with such undoubted talent. At the time all I could do was move on and think about the season ahead, but I later found out that the effect of not getting Robert and Gavin, together with Stuart's departure, were all things which began to trigger concerns in Steve Gibson's mind.

I got on well with Steve and still do to this day. He has always been very honest and forthright in the way he goes about his business, and even at that time had a clearly defined vision of what he wanted for Middlesbrough Football Club. During the course of the season that vision and determination would bring him into conflict with Colin Henderson, and in the second half of the campaign the chairman stepped down. The 'power struggle' at boardroom level as it was often referred to, was something else I could have done without. One of the consequences was that from October through to the following March there were no board meetings and this was at a crucial time for the club and for me as a manager of a newly promoted team battling away in the Premiership. Although I failed to get Gavin and Robert, players did come into the club, like defenders Derek Whyte and Chris Morris from Celtic, while Andy Payton went in the other direction, and I bought Craig Hignett from Crewe at the end of November.

We began the season quite well and only lost twice in our first eight league games, but then only won once in our next eight. We were still just below mid-table at the end of December, but then came two months that destroyed us and we had a terrible time in January and February, winning only one game and the pressure began to build. At the start of March we were in 21ˢᵗ place. We rallied a little towards the end of the season winning three and drawing one of our last six matches, but it wasn't enough to save us. One of the games we lost during those last six matches was at Palace 4-1, and they thought they'd done enough to keep their own heads above water with the win, but in the end were relegated with us on 49 points. We finished with 44 and Forest were bottom four points behind.

It was a huge disappointment compared to the euphoria of the season before, when I'd been chaired around the pitch by supporters at Molineux, but we simply weren't good enough to stay up. What I did realise was that there was a much bigger expectation level than I'd experienced at Charlton. When I'd got promotion with them it was almost seen as a bonus, at Middlesbrough I was expected to get them up and keep them up. I did the first part, but couldn't do the second.

The key in the first year when we'd got promotion was the passion of so many of the players I'd inherited at the club, coupled with man-management, coaching and organisation. It saw us through a tough season and got us up, probably sooner than I'd anticipated, and I think it was a real achievement by everyone involved to do what we did.

After relegation I knew it was going to be a case of having to get rid of some of the players and bringing others through. My own feeling was that it was going to be a season of consolidation, with the intention of maybe having a real crack at promotion the following year. There had been rumblings from some fans who weren't happy with me but I think the majority recognised what had happened and could see that having been relegated it might not be a case of a quick return.

Lennie

I was told by the board that I had to raise funds which I was no stranger to, having gone through all of those tough financial years at Charlton. I knew it meant that the first realistic offers I got for some of the squad were going to have to be taken. Out went Jimmy Phillips to Bolton and Willie Falconer to Sheffield United for around £650,000 and then, early in the season, I did a really good piece of business for the club by selling Kernaghan to Manchester City for £1.6 million. Not a bad return on a player who had cost absolutely nothing and who had nearly left for Charlton two years earlier for £300,000, but he was also a player I knew we would miss. There were other departures as well and that meant having to bring some of our young kids into the team. Some of them like full-back Richard Liburd and winger Alan Moore were real talents.

After four straight wins we were at the top of the table early on and we stayed in the promotion places until early November, but by the end of the year we had gone on a run which saw us record just one victory in nine matches. January was really no better as we struggled to put anything together and fell to 16th place in the table. We got a couple of important wins in February which lifted the spirits a little, and off the field there was a hugely significant change in the boardroom, when Steve Gibson finally became the club's chairman.

There had been on-going talks about plans to move the club to a new stadium for the start of the 1995-96 season, and Steve Gibson was the man who had been pushing for such a move. Colin Henderson had been much more conservative in his outlook and vision for Middlesbrough, but Gibson very definitely felt the future of the club lay away from Ayresome Park at a new purpose built stadium. Between him and ICI, who were represented by a guy called George Cooke, they held 52 per cent of the shares while another man named Henry Moszkowicz held the remaining shares. Apparently Gibson and Moszkowicz were poles apart when it came to the direction they wanted the club to go in, and eventually Steve bought Henry's shares and became chairman, with Colin Henderson stepping down from the board. It meant Steve Gibson could push ahead with his plans, and as well as Cooke, he also had the support of the two other directors, Graham Fordy and Reg Corbidge.

Once Steve took over as chairman I began to have more contact with him and I could see he was very keen to really move the club forward. What I didn't realise at the time, but know now, is that although he liked me as a person, it seems that by the time he took over he'd already made up his mind I wasn't the man he wanted as manager. He has gone on record as saying that even by the Christmas of 1993, he was already looking for a new manager.

I can honestly say I had no idea about this at the time, and my main concern was making sure we battled through and could really have a go at it in the next season. The home crowds had dipped and there had been some chants and boos from the fans. There was also speculation in the press, but it was something I had to live with. I must admit that towards the end of the season I had a feeling all was not well and I might be in trouble. I said as much to John Pickering, and being the fantastic bloke he was, John suggested that if he offered to go it might give me more breathing space. It was typical of him, but I told him that if anyone was going it was me, and given the tremendous job he'd done for Middlesbrough, I felt the club should keep hold of him, which was actually what they did.

I wasn't surprised when I was finally given the bullet, only by the timing of it. I didn't see it coming and thought I would see the season out and then maybe get fired in the summer, or half way through the next season if things hadn't picked up. But after our last home game of the season, which we lost 3-2 against Palace, they wheeled me in and gave me the news. Keith Lamb came to get me after the match and Steve Gibson told me they were terminating my contract. After 12 years as a manager I'd been sacked for the first time.

11

JUST THE JOB

My first reaction after being given the news was to ask them a question.

"What are you going to do now?" I asked.

It may sound like a strange reaction to being given the news that you were no longer wanted, but I wasn't in a state of shock and could still think clearly. I had genuine affection for the club and great respect for Steve Gibson. I'd put a lot into my time at Middlesbrough and to this day I believe I played my part in helping them move forward.

I had to accept the fact that Steve and the board didn't think I was the right man to take them to the next level. I could understand that. Steve had a vision of what he believed should be the club's future and part of that was attracting a different manager to lead the club. I had no problem with that, and I let Steve Gibson and Keith Lamb know I completely understood where they were coming from. That's life, and to be fair to them they handled the whole thing very well, and there was never any of the sort of financial wrangling you often hear of when a manager leaves a club.

Steve Gibson asked me who I thought might be best suited to the job. They had already done their home work and narrowed down the possible candidates to just a couple of people, one of them was Bryan Robson. I thought Robbo could be just right for them and what they had in mind for the club. The move to a new stadium was in the pipeline and scheduled for the summer of 1995, there was going to be money to spend for the new man, Bryan Robson had a certain stature in the game and his name alone was bound to put more on the gate. For quite a lot of reasons it sounded right to me and I offered to do my bit by going to see Robbo myself.

It may seem strange now, but the fact was at that time I could open doors for them that they couldn't. Steve was still young and relatively new to being a football club chairman, but I'd been around for a while and was friends with Alex Ferguson. I'd got to know him quite well over the years and knew him from his days in Scotland because, of those scouting trips I made north of the border, which had resulted in some very good buys during my time at Charlton. I was a pretty frequent visitor up there and remember once meeting Ken Bates, who was then the Chelsea chairman, at the Scottish Cup final.

"What are you doing here?" he asked me as we took our seats. "You can't afford any of these players!"

I also recall once having a conversation with Fergie at a hotel near Glasgow airport after I'd been on another scouting mission the night before with Jimmy Hill, and I told Alex that if he was going to make the move south, then there were only two clubs he could possibly move to, Liverpool or Manchester United. He'd already done brilliantly in Scotland with Aberdeen and it was inevitable that at some stage in the not too distant future, one of the big English clubs would want him to be their manager. I had that conversation with him in 1985 and in November 1986 he became United's manager.

After taking over at United we stayed in touch and sometimes went to games together, as we did for a play-off match between Blackburn and Crystal Palace in 1989. Typically, Alex had told me to meet him after the long drive north and invited me to have something to eat at his house before we both went off to the game. In the end I was late getting to him but he doubled back to pick me up and then we both watched the match.

He was and is a football man through and through and his knowledge of the game and players is quite incredible. Some people ask whether you have to be a great man to be a great manager like Sir Alex, and my feeling is that you do, and he is.

To just give some idea of the measure of the man I'd like to recall an incident back in November 1994. Alex was already proving to be a huge success with United and I had been invited along to a charity lunch in Manchester at which he was due to speak. The night before United had played a European Cup match in Barcelona and had been thumped 4-0. He hadn't got back until about four in the morning, but turned up for the lunch when other people might have made their excuses and not bothered. Just to add to the day, I had arranged to go and watch United's reserves that night and Alex insisted on coming along and made sure I was looked after. He must have been out on his feet by this time, and I think he actually went and had a kip in the dressing room during the game! But that's the sort of character he is. There was no way he would have thought of missing the charity event having given his word that he would be there, and there was no way he was going to go home without making sure I was looked after at the game.

I was one of a handful of league managers to be invited to his testimonial in 1997, and it was a privilege to be asked to attend. Not only is he a remarkable football manager, he is also an extremely decent bloke who has been a huge help not only to me, but also to many other people both in and out of the game over the years.

Back in May 1994, United were already on their way to a second successive Premier League title which would see them qualify for the European Cup and that game against Barcelona. They were due to play Southampton in a midweek game at Old Trafford in their penultimate league game of the season. I phoned Alex up and told him that

Middlesbrough were keen on getting Bryan Robson as my replacement, and that I'd said I would be happy to speak to Robbo on their behalf.

As ever Alex was as helpful as could be. He invited me to the game and I had a pre-match meal with him and his staff, he then said I could use his office to sit down with Bryan and have a chat to him. When I spoke to Robbo I told him that becoming the new Middlesbrough manager would be a great opportunity for him. I said it was a brilliant place, that he'd probably have £2 million or £3 million to spend, and that there were some good young players there. I also explained that he'd never be in a stronger position than when he started. I explained that having the name he did in the game would automatically increase the attendances and also said he had a great chance of getting them up in his first season. I gave him a bit of background on Steve Gibson and said what a good bloke he was, which may have sounded a bit strange seeing as he'd sacked me three days earlier, but I meant it. The plans Steve had for a new stadium and the direction he wanted the club to take sounded superb. It wasn't so much that I was trying to sell the club to Bryan, it was more a case of laying out in front of him just what a great opportunity it was in his first managerial job. He already had Coventry and Wolves after him, but I honestly thought Middlesbrough would be right for him

I'd done my bit by talking to Robbo and the next stage was down to Steve Gibson. I arranged to meet Bryan two days later at Wetherby, but he was an hour late and I was beginning to think there might be something wrong. When he did arrive he followed me to a Little Chef on the A19, where I'd said I would meet Keith Lamb and the plan was for him to then take Bryan to see Steve Gibson at a rather grand place called Wilton Castle.

We drove to the Little Chef, I said hello to Keith and then goodbye to him and Robbo as they headed off to see Steve. With that my involvement with Middlesbrough ended. It had been fantastic for the first 18 months and a hard slog for the second part of my time there, but always enjoyable. I loved the experience and still have great affection for the club and their fans. I also have great respect for Steve Gibson and what he has done. He has rightly earned praise for the way he has run the club and for the way he has consistently backed the managers who have worked for him. The club has moved on and things have changed a lot since I was there including the fact that the old ground is now a housing development. Whenever I drive past now I look across and see someone's bedroom window in the spot where my old office used to be. I still get on well with Steve Gibson and I have a good relationship with the club to this day. I also like Middlesbrough and the surrounding countryside, so much so that I can see myself perhaps buying a place up there one day.

As I left Keith and Bryan that day I knew life had to go on. Being sacked was a new experience for me, but I didn't intend to sit around moping on what had happened. I was a football manager and I wanted to find a football club to manage. What I ended up doing was making the only real professional mistake of my career.

In hindsight what I should have done after leaving Middlesbrough was to take six months off, or at least, that's probably what I needed to do. But my only thought at the time was that I felt I needed to keep working. It was something in me, maybe the way I'd been brought up, but whatever it was I just wanted to get a job again as quickly as I could. It was the first time I'd been sacked and I'd been a manager for 12 years. That's a long time and of course it was a very new experience for me.

From the very first day I'd thrown myself into the job at Middlesbrough. It was new and very exciting. Moving from one end of the country to the other hadn't bothered me, even though the change in lifestyle eventually took a toll on my marriage to Lyn, and things just didn't work out between us, with her deciding to move back down south. It's often easy to forget all the knock-on effects being a football manager can have. It's easy to immerse yourself in a new job and it becomes all-consuming, but a manager's wife and family are suddenly thrown into a completely different world and it can be very difficult on those people around you.

I honestly don't think the full effect of getting the sack hit me until some time later, and there are moments when you start to wonder why it happened and perhaps even begin to question yourself. If I'd taken time to sit back, take some time off and readjust, I think it would have been better for me, but doing that just wasn't in my make-up and so I started to think of the future and tried to be as positive about it as I could.

At the end of a season there is always a change-around at clubs, with managers coming and going, but that particular summer there were few jobs on offer. In fact, there were probably only about four that came up as the close season began and I ended up being in the frame for all of them. One was at Lincoln, one at Fulham where Jimmy Hill was chairman and he rang me up to see if I was interested, then there were vacancies at Barnsley and Bradford.

A little less than three weeks after I'd been sacked at Middlesbrough, I got a call from John Pickering who had been such a fantastic assistant to me while I'd been at Ayresome Park. He told me that the Bradford chairman, Geoffrey Richmond, would be interested in talking to me about the manager's job at the club. Frank Stapleton had been in charge of Bradford, but he'd been sacked on the same day as I left Middlesbrough. I had a meeting with Richmond and he seemed keen on me becoming the new manager. It was nice to feel wanted again, especially so soon after being given the elbow, and after pretty much agreeing terms I shook hands with him on the deal and drove home.

The next day I got a phone call from the Barnsley chairman, John

Dennis, who was a man I greatly admired and respected. He asked me if I would be interested in becoming their new manager. Viv Anderson had been in charge, but had left to become Bryan Robson's assistant when he'd said yes to Middlesbrough. Barnsley were a league above Bradford, who were in Division Two, but I explained to John that I'd already shaken hands with Geoffrey Richmond and couldn't go back on it.

John phoned me five times in all that day trying to get me to change my mind. I hadn't actually signed anything with Bradford, but I just felt it wasn't right to change my mind at the last moment. When you think of what goes on every day in football it was perhaps naïve of me. I should have been a bit more ruthless about the whole thing, because I know I would have ended up being happier working with John. Barnsley appointed Danny Wilson as their manager and a few years later, were promoted to the Premier League. I'm not saying I would have achieved the same level of success with them, but I'm sure it would have been an interesting experience managing them and working with John.

In fact, there was another chance to manage a club that summer after I'd already shaken hands on the Bradford job. It was never a real possibility as far as I was concerned and involved a side in Cyprus. I was asked to go over for a visit that had already been set up, and I went more out of curiosity than anything else. I travelled out with the agent who was hoping to set the whole thing up and when we got to the ground we were given our tickets which looked as though they were in the director's box. At half-time we were standing up having a look around when a guy came over and threw a punch at someone sitting a few rows in front. Suddenly there was chaos all around us and I thought we weren't in the director's box after all, but I was wrong. The fight had started when the other club's chairman came over and threw a punch at his opposite number! I'd seen a lot in football but that was a first.

Lennie

So instead of heading off to Cyprus or Barnsley, I became the new Bradford manager and can honestly say that within a matter of weeks both Geoffrey Richmond and I knew it had been a big mistake. We just weren't right for each other and certainly didn't see eye to eye on things, but I'd signed a three year contract and we were both kind of locked in to having to work with each other. He was a very clever man and financially very shrewd. He was also very demanding of your time, and one of those people who is in early and goes home late. Despite knowing even before a ball was kicked in anger at the start of the new season that I'd made a huge mistake, there was nothing I could really do other than get on with the job of managing Bradford.

We had a decent start to the campaign and were third at the end of September with Paul Jewell doing particularly well and scoring 11 league goals in nine games, but couldn't maintain those results and began to slide down the league. By the end of the season we were in 14th place and probably my biggest achievement was the fact that I'd managed to sell one of our best players and in doing so made the club a lot of money.

That may sound strange but it's also part of the reality of life as a football manager. The fact was that Dean Richards was an extremely good central defender who was attracting interest from some of the bigger clubs. One of them was Wolves who were going for promotion in Division One. I encouraged Wolves to take Dean on loan which basically entailed us getting a loan fee of £250,000. In effect what that meant was that if Dean went to them on a permanent basis there would be the usual transfer fee, but if they took him on loan and decided not to go through with a transfer, Bradford would still get £250,000. They took Dean on loan for the rest of that season and although they missed out in the play-off semi-finals against Bolton, their manager, Graham Taylor, was keen to sign the player in the summer of 1995. Geoffrey Richmond let me take care of the transfer negotiations, which I took as a compliment, and we ended up with a fantastic deal which saw Richards go for a total of £1,850,000. Our league position might have been disappointing, but in financial terms I think I did pretty well for the club that season, because any side in Division Two as it was then, would have been extremely grateful for that sort of cash injection.

We were unbeaten in our first four league matches at the start of the following season and only had two defeats in the first eight games. But by the time we went to Brentford at the end of November the picture had changed and we were looking for only our second win in eight games. We lost 2-1 and were poor. Two days later on the Monday, Geoffrey called me into his office and it was clear we'd reached the end of the road. The form had been disappointing, we were in 11th place in the table and he was getting a bit of stick from some of the fans.

"What do you think I should do?" he asked me.

I told him that I thought he had two options. Firstly we could bat on for another month and see if things turned around, or he could do something straight away and we could part company. I don't think it was a difficult decision for either of us. I certainly don't think I damaged the club in any way. At the end of that season Chris Kamara, having stepped up from being my assistant to take over as manager, led Bradford to promotion after a 2-0 play-off final win against Notts County at Wembley. I like to think I played some part, because it was pretty much the squad I left them with. So almost 13 years to the day since I'd taken over as manager of Charlton I found myself out of work for the second time in 18 months. Looking back now I'm sure going to Barnsley would have been the better option.

I have two mottos that I have lived by during the course of my career and in my life. The first is, 'never look back wishing,' the second is almost an inevitable one for any manager, and that is, 'take risks.' Those thoughts were certainly in my mind when I was given the chance of another job a matter of weeks after leaving Bradford.

After four and a half years in the north it was time for me to head south once again.

12

THE HATTERS FIT

Looking back on my time with Bradford I have to say there was a real sense of relief on my part when it was all over. Don't misunderstand me, there's nothing wrong with the club and the supporters were fine until a few of them started to make a bit of a noise towards the end of my stay there. But as I've mentioned, I knew pretty early on that I'd made a big mistake. I did the job professionally and certainly did no harm to the club during my time with them it was just the wrong move for me.

I jumped into a job too quickly after the Middlesbrough experience and didn't know at the time how getting the sack at Ayresome Park would have a much deeper effect on me than I could ever have imagined. I think I also perhaps made a mistake at the end of that first season. Maybe I should have flipped things and made Chris Kamara the manager, while taking more of a back seat in a slightly detached role. It might have worked better for me and for him at the time, who knows? The one thing I did realise was that when Geoffrey Richmond had that conversation with me it was clear he wanted a parting of the ways just as much as I did. I think it was more a case of him reacting to what had gone on in that last month or so before I left, and perhaps listening to some disgruntled fans.

It wasn't the same scenario I'd experienced at Middlesbrough where Steve Gibson had a clear plan and vision for what he wanted at the club, but whatever way you looked at both of those jobs the fact remained that as Christmas approached in 1995 I found myself out of work, but once again it wasn't to be for very long, which happily, has basically turned out to be the case throughout my career.

A week before Christmas Terry Westley parted company with Luton after only five months in charge. He was a young coach who had already been at the club working with the youth players, and when David Pleat left to take over as manager of Sheffield Wednesday during the summer of 1995, Terry got the chance to succeed him. He'd been allowed to spend quite a lot of money assembling a squad and had forked out something approaching £2 million in the transfer market, which was a huge amount for the size of the club. It was ambitious but things just hadn't worked out for him, which sometimes happens in management. By the time he left Luton, they were adrift at the bottom of Division One or what is now the Championship, with just four wins from 22 league games. It was going to be a tough job for any manager that went in, but then when you're out of work and get the chance to step back in, it's seldom anything but a tough job, or there wouldn't have been a vacancy in the first place.

I travelled down to Luton for a meeting with David Kohler, who was their chairman and managing director. The chat I had with him went well and I outlined what I thought should be done and what I brought to the job if they wanted to take me on board. It must have gone well, because he later asked me to stay on and meet the rest of the directors that evening, so by the end of the day I knew I was in with a very decent chance of getting the job, although I also realised I wasn't the only candidate.

I think at that stage Luton were looking for a safe pair of hands, in what was obviously a very tricky situation. There was no doubt that whoever took over was going to have their work cut out in trying to prevent the club from slipping down a division, but I was certainly no stranger to tough situations at football clubs and although it was difficult I wasn't daunted by the thought of becoming the new manager.

David Kohler and his board clearly wanted to make a quick decision on the appointment and it wasn't too long after speaking to them that I got a call to say they wanted me to join the club. It was a good move for me and I was happy to be back in football so quickly. It meant relocating again, but that wasn't really too much of a problem, because I'd kept my house in Kent, and in many ways it was like coming home. The person who probably noticed the biggest change was my new partner, Jenny, who I met in my closing months at Middlesbrough, but she was pleased for me and very supportive despite the fact that I knew it would involve a change in lifestyle for her.

My first game in charge came two days before Christmas when we entertained fifth placed Huddersfield at Kenilworth Road. Luton had lost their previous two matches, but they performed well on the day and earned a very decent 2-2 draw. We then had three games postponed which meant our next match was in the Third Round of the FA Cup, and we got walloped 7-1 at Grimsby. Despite that terrible result the players began to respond, and we went on a seven game unbeaten run in the league, winning five of them. It meant we were able to lift ourselves off the bottom and were in 19th place by the end of February, but that was just about as good as it got. In the end it was too much for us and with some key players suffering injuries during the crucial last part of the season, we simply weren't able to stay up. I think a lot of people were hopeful that we were going to make it, but the truth was the team just wasn't good enough. It had started to look like a daunting task during the last couple of months of the season and the reality was that I then had to start thinking of how we were going to cope with the drop.

It's never easy for any club when they are relegated and having been there before, I knew that one of the realities of life when it happens is having to cut your playing cloth accordingly. The good thing from my point of view was that we managed to keep most of the squad together, although I did sell Scott Oakes to David Pleat at Sheffield Wednesday for £450,000. Luton were also blessed with having a fine crop of kids coming through and it was something the club had managed to do long before I went there. It continued during my time as manager and also after I left, which is remarkable for a club of its size, with far less facilities than a lot of other teams.

I re-jigged things during the summer and at the start of the new season after we'd lost our first three matches. We then won three on the bounce and went on a run which saw us lose just one game in 14 league matches. It took us to fifth place in the table by November with things beginning to look a lot brighter for us, and by the turn of the year we were second in the league. One of the reasons for our position was the goal scoring of Tony Thorpe, who had been playing on the left and I moved him inside and pushed him up front where he had a fantastic time, scoring 31 goals in all that season, 28 of which were in league matches. Despite his goals we couldn't quite make an automatic promotion spot and finished the season in third place.

It meant another taste of the play-off for me and we met a very good Crewe side in the semi-final over two legs. We'd beaten them 6-0 in the league during the previous December, but they had some quality players in their ranks including the likes of Danny Murphy, and the play-off games were a different affair. We lost the first leg 2-1 at their place and then could only draw 2-2 at home in the second game, going out 4-3 on aggregate.

Towards the end of the season we had run out of bodies and it cost us. With six games to go we slipped out of the top two and just weren't able to make it over the line, which was a real shame because it would have been great to bounce straight back. Instead it became a bit of a struggle with financial issues always a problem. As a manager you obviously want success on the pitch, but it's not always just about that. There's a responsibility that comes with the job and that means trying to look after the club's money when it comes to transfer dealings. I had always done that during my career and to me it was second nature. I soon became aware that there wasn't much money to spend in the transfer market. It was more about how well I could do when it came to selling some of the players we already had at the club, and someone who was sold at the end of that season for very big money wasn't even an established first team player.

I mentioned the fact that Luton as a club have produced some exceptional playing talent over the years, and I could see that was the case when I took over. There were some very good kids who had come through and also some who were on the verge of playing first team football. One youngster was still essentially a youth player, but you didn't have to be a genius to recognise the fact that he was clearly going to make it at the very highest level of the game. His name was Matthew Upson and near the start of that season after relegation he was one of the substitutes in our 1-0 home win over Rotherham. He didn't really figure at first team level again during the season, but by the end of it he had become an Arsenal player and we had taken £1 million from his transfer. It was an exceptional piece of business for us, but at the same time I knew that Arsène Wenger had bought an exceptional young player. It wasn't just Arsenal who were after Matthew because he was due to go and see Kenny Dalglish at Newcastle, but they had a bit of fixture congestion and he never actually went up there. Instead he went along to Arsenal and that was it, they knew he was a real talent and they weren't going to let him out of their grasp. Although it didn't quite happen for him at Arsenal, he's gone on to show his quality for Birmingham, West Ham and England. There were others at the club who later went on to have good careers in the Premiership, like Matty Taylor and Emmerson Boyce, as well as Matthew Spring who has had a great league career.

Apart from the financial issues that were increasingly part of my job, I also realised it wasn't all plain sailing when it came to the boardroom. David Kohler was the chairman, but there was another guy called, Cliff Bassett, who had a lot of money in the club. I got on well with him and with David, but it was clear at times that the two of them didn't always see eye to eye. I spent a lot of time at board meetings, and tried to manage the two sides. That can often happen and being a football manager isn't just about managing the team, it is also about the way you manage your chairman and the board at the club you're working for.

At Bradford I knew within a few weeks that I wasn't right for Geoffrey Richmond and he wasn't right for me. You can never expect to have a perfectly smooth relationship with a chairman, but if you can't get on and work with him then there's going to be a problem. I can honestly say that I still get on with all the people I have worked for over the years, and whatever differences I might have had with them at times, I think they all realised that I tried to do the best I could for their club.

In the case of Luton it was a hard slog from the start, and although we just missed out in the play-offs, I was aware that trying to go one better the next season was going to be virtually impossible. We were ill-equipped from a playing point of view and we struggled for most of the season, eventually finishing in 17th place.

Once again financial practicalities were also a part of what was going on and two of our better players were sold. Ceri Hughes went to Wimbledon for £400,000 in the summer, and then in February 1998 Tony Thorpe went to Fulham for £800,000. He had been the top scorer the season before, and even though he departed with 15 league games to go, he still ended up top scorer for us again, with 17 goals, 14 of them in Division Two.

When things like that happen fans are understandably upset, particularly when the team isn't doing too well in the league. But I was trying to perform a balancing act, and the bottom line was always going to be that the finances had to be taken care of as best I could. It was clear pretty early on in that season that I wasn't exactly flavour of the month with some of the fans. We played Watford at home in a local derby at the beginning of October and got thumped 4-0. Quite naturally our fans were none too happy and one of them even ran onto the pitch to let his feelings be known. We were one off the bottom of the table at the time, which also didn't help matters. But sometimes it's difficult for fans to appreciate what you're doing or having to cope with as you try to manage their club. I accepted fully that it was my responsibility to send out teams that could do well on the pitch, and also that I needed to be very careful with the club finances.

It wasn't all one-way traffic and I was able to bring some players in on permanent moves and also loan deals. One of the most successful loans during that 1997-98 season, came at the tail end of it when we were really struggling near the bottom of the table. By this time David Pleat was the director of football at Tottenham and they had a 20-year-old striker named Rory Allen. Once again I was running out of bodies and I managed to get Rory on transfer deadline day. He scored on his debut for us in the 3-2 away win at Walsall, and played in all the remaining games of the season, ending up with six goals in eight games, which was a tremendous contribution and helped to make sure we stayed up.

Having flirted with relegation the next season was an improvement in terms of where we eventually finished and there were also kids coming through, but we still never managed to sustain any kind of real push for promotion despite being in the top six for most of the first three months. We finished the campaign in 12th place, but perhaps the most significant events for the club took place in the second half of the season. In February David Kohler, who had taken an enormous amount of stick from the fans over the years, decided to stand down. He'd also apparently had a petrol bomb and matches posted through his letterbox around the same time. Once again he and Cliff seemed to be at loggerheads and a month later in March 1999, the club was put into administration. As manager I knew it was important to work closely with the administrator. It's something I have always told young managers to do if they are in a similar situation, because it not only helps the administrator, it also allows you to be involved more closely and to keep tabs on what is happening on a daily basis. One of the things that needed to be done during that summer was to bring money into the club by selling players. Of course the administrator had the right to do that but at the same time they don't have the sort of knowledge someone working in the game would have and I told them that if there were players to be sold, I could do it because I thought I would be able to get the right sort of price. Graham Alexander was sold to Preston for £50,000 and Sean Evers to Reading for £500,000 before the season ended. In the summer I sold Kelvin Davis for £600,000 and Chris Willmott for £350,000 to Wimbledon.

Again it was probably not what fans wanted to see happening at their club, but the point was there was no guarantee there would be a club at all as the 1999-2000 season approached. In the end it was Cliff Bassett who came to the rescue with about five minutes to go before the start of the new season, digging deep into his own pocket to effectively take control of the club.

It was cutting it fine, but then I'd been used to all the High Court stuff with Charlton, and learned that there was nothing I could do about it. I just had to wait and see what happened. Had Luton not come out of administration before the start of the season, they would have been thrown out of the league. The good thing about the whole period of about six months in administration was that nobody lost their job or got fired because of the position the club found itself in.

Once again we had a decent start to the season and there was probably a sense of relief all round after what had happened, but the squad wasn't good enough to mount a serious challenge for promotion and we finished 13th. I'd had some of the fans on my back during the course of the campaign and it had pretty much been like that for about 18 months or more. It wasn't an easy job but I was happy to soldier on in what were never the easiest of circumstances. I didn't have lots of players to call on, and once again I had cause to be grateful for the fact that the club had managed to produce some decent home grown talent, because quite often eight or nine of them would make up my squad on a Saturday afternoon.

At the end of the season Cliff Bassett decided to sell his controlling stake in the club to a man named Mike Watson-Challis who had been a director at Luton from the mid-1980's until the early 1990's. I had a couple of meetings with him during the course of the summer and each time he repeated a phrase to me when it came to talking about the club.

"It's you and me against the world sunshine," he said.

I found this a bit odd, but thought he was trying to say we both had a tough job but we had to get on with it. That was fine with me, but the third time I was summoned it was for a meeting with the new financial manager, who told me that the club had decided to make a change.

After four and a half years I was out. I knew I hadn't been popular with the fans for the last couple of seasons. Maybe I was a bit too honest and told them a few home truths, or perhaps it was the selling of players. In fact, one of the last things I had done in the season which had just ended, was to sell another promising player, Gary Doherty, to Tottenham. I sat in a room with Cliff Bassett, David Pleat and Sir Alan Sugar to sort out the deal, and we ended up selling him for £1 million, plus various add-ons linked to games, sell-on fees and possible international appearances.

It was another good deal for Luton, but another player lost as far as a lot of supporters were concerned. It was also part of my remit to strike the best deal I could and although I might not go down as one of the most popular managers in Luton's history with the fans, I feel I did a good job in often very difficult circumstances, while at the same time making them a net transfer profit of something approaching £5 million. Even if I say so myself, I think that is a masterpiece of financial management, and I certainly feel I can hold my head up when it comes to the part I played in trying to make sure the club had a decent future, which is why it's so sad to see them no longer in league football.

I was replaced by one of the club's famous old boys, Ricky Hill. Half way through the following season with the club struggling near the foot of the table he parted company with Luton. Former Wimbledon manager, Joe Kinnear, was appointed but couldn't halt the slide and Luton found themselves relegated to the bottom division of the Football League.

On the day I was given the bullet, I was standing on a platform at Luton station waiting for a train on my way home, when I got a call on my mobile phone. As usual I'd been looking at the transfer market and had a player called Linvoy Primus, who was leaving Reading and has since played in the Premier League with Portsmouth, lined up as a possible target. I'd mentioned this to Cliff Bassett and when I answered the phone I discovered it was him on the other end.

"How did you get on with the player you were after?" he asked.

"Haven't you heard Cliff?" I said. "I've just been sacked!"

13

FROM PUERTO BANUS TO CLEETHORPES

For the first time in 23 years I found myself uninvolved in any pre-season preparations. It felt very strange and I wasn't really sure what to do with myself. In the end I decided to try and keep involved in the game as best I could and went off to watch other managers in action with their clubs. I went up and stayed with Burnley manager Stan Ternent for a few days and then went over to see my old mate Roy Hodgson, who was working in Copenhagen. I went to about three or four different places in all, which was novel, but not quite like being involved yourself.

I also did a bit of media work for a television channel called, Boro TV, who I'd previously worked for. They were a cable network who, as the name might suggest, covered all things to do with Middlesbrough football club. I'd worked for them helping with commentary on matches when Middlesbrough had played games in London, and that summer they asked if I wanted to go out to Gibraltar because Middlesbrough were playing some friendly matches nearby. We were based in the same hotel as the team and it was a funny experience seeing it all from the point of view of the media, rather than as manager of the club. Robbo was still the man in charge and was as good as gold, not just with me, but with everyone covering the trip and one of my fellow Boro TV colleagues was Bernie Slaven. We might have had our run-ins when I managed the club, but we buried the hatchet, and got on fine throughout the trip.

Lennie

On the day before the new season was due to start I was in Spain, strolling around Puerto Banus looking at the expensive yachts and boats. Lovely though it all was, I couldn't help wondering to myself what I was doing there. I was a football man, the season was just around the corner, and I was wandering around Puerto Banus on my own. Two weeks later I was walking along the seafront at Cleethorpes!

Like I've said things can happen quickly in football, and once again that was the case when I became manager of Grimsby Town. They had started the season with a defeat and a draw prompting the board to sack Alan Buckley, making him the earliest managerial casualty of the season. It's a fact of life that as a manager you tend to get a job because another manager has been sacked. Obviously it is never nice if you are on the receiving end and are the one being given the boot, but if it's a case of being the man a club want as their new manager, then you have to see it as an opportunity and try to make the most of it. That is the nature of the business and we all have to get on with it.

I settled into life very quickly at Grimsby, renting a bungalow in a lovely little market town not too far away, and getting stuck into the day to day business of looking after the team. My assistant was a guy named John Cockerill, who had been there as a coach and player, and had also worked alongside Alan Buckley. Once again I was blessed with having someone alongside me who I could trust and get on with. At Luton I'd had Wayne Turner and then John Moore.

When I first arrived at Grimsby John Cockerill came to see me and said that he'd understand if I wanted to bring in my own staff, but I was happy to have John there and the more I got to know him the more I came to appreciate and like him. The best way to describe what he was like is to say that the words honesty and integrity were made for him.

I soon found out that Grimsby were a really nice little club. They were in Division One, which was a great achievement for them, because they were by no means a big outfit and I realised that my main task was to make sure they maintained their status and remained in the division.

At about this time ITV digital had been formed and they had promised to inject around £315 million into the Football League over a period of three years as they showed the games from all three leagues. The teams in Division One were going to get a bigger fee each year than those in the Second Division and, in turn, they got more than teams in Division Three. The money was seen as a huge financial help to clubs, and Grimsby wanted to make sure they were safe at the end of the season, which would mean a big cash injection and a big part of the finances for a club of their size, with an average gate of around 6,000.

I was quickly aware that although we had some good players at the club, there weren't enough of them. I needed to get some bodies into the squad to make sure we stayed afloat and didn't sink into the Second Division. After getting promotion two years earlier they had finished a very good 11th in the table at the end of their first season, but had battled in the second year finishing in 20th place.

As soon as I saw what the situation was I decided to try and add to the squad as best I could. Financially there just wasn't the cash to go on a spending spree in the transfer market. I also realised that the club probably didn't want to be saddled with long-term contracts for new players, and so I went for loan signings.

At the time I had quite a few good contacts abroad and I used some of them to bring in players who I thought could do a good job in the short term, and at the same time ensure that the club remained safe in Division One. I went back to Roy Hodgson in Denmark and got a player called David Nielsen. I spoke to another old mate, Bobby Houghton, who had been the Chinese national coach and was still in the country working with a club side. Thanks to his advice I took a centre-half named Zhang Enhua, who was the captain of China, and from other contacts I also picked up a Norwegian left-back called Knut Fostervold, and a Dutch midfielder named Menno Willems. It was a different direction for the club to go in and a bit novel, because I don't think there'd been too many Chinese centre-halves at Grimsby in the past! Although it was by no means cheap, it was certainly a lot less expensive than spending heavily in the transfer market, which is what we would have had to do in order to get the right quality of player we needed, and at the end of it all my justification was the cash that would be forthcoming from the digital deal if we stayed in the division.

We battled our way through the season and there was no doubt it was a slog, but at the same time I found it an enjoyable slog. I liked the club, I liked the people I was working for and the fans were good. Towards the end of the season nearly all the loan signings had gone, and we found ourselves very near the bottom. In the end it came down to another last day of drama. Of course, it was the sort of thing I'd experienced before in my career, and as we went into our final game at home to Fulham we knew exactly what we had to do – win and we'd stay up.

Fulham were head and shoulders above anyone else in the league and had already won the championship, amassing 101 points in the process. On paper it looked pretty bleak for us, but on that last day of the season we had a lot more to play for than Fulham and in the end it showed.

Paul Groves gave us the lead after 27 minutes of the match and that was the way it stayed. Cheered on by 8,706 fans, which was our biggest gate of the season, we hung on for a famous victory and with it secured our place in the division for another season. When I look back on that season now, I genuinely think it was a real feat and the odds were against us right through, but the players did a great job, and the loan signings I made played a real part in the whole thing.

As I headed off on holiday before preparing for a new season I was pretty happy and contented to be at the club, but as so often happens in football, changes were just around the corner. During that summer there were moves in the boardroom, with chairman Doug Everitt leaving. He had been instrumental in bringing me to the club along with the vice chairman, Brian Huxford, and when things changed I knew it was going to affect me. I was actually called back from holiday to discuss the way the club were going to operate in the future. They were talking about making cuts here and there and being careful, although in the July of that summer we actually ended up paying out £150,000 to Everton for Phil Jevons, but I still got the feeling things weren't going to be easy for me and that the writing was on the wall. It soon became clear that was the case and we weren't really thinking along the same lines.

On the playing side we did alright early on and we were second in the league early in September, but form dipped alarmingly after that and by the time we lost 1-0 at home against Coventry on Boxing Day, we'd only won once in 20 league matches and were one off the bottom.

It was a poor run and although we weren't getting hammered each week, we weren't winning either. Two days later on a Friday morning I was called in and given the sack. It was all done in a very professional way and in fairness to them they made it clear that there was nothing personal in their decision, but it still left me without a job. It was bad enough for me, but regrettably John Cockerill became a victim and lost his job as well. I admit that we'd had a terrible run, but as a manager you realise that not everyone can win trophies. I have always said that you should judge a manager by the way he leaves the club he's been in charge of, and the fact was that during my 16 months at the club I'd managed to make sure they retained their status in Division One, which was the paramount concern when I went there.

I went back to my bungalow, threw a few bags into the back of my car and headed south for my home in Kent. It was quite a long drive back and on the way I naturally began to wonder what was going to happen next. It wasn't quite like losing your job at the end of a season when you know there are going to be changes at other clubs and there might be the possibility of a job. I'd been sacked three days before the New Year and with all the holiday fixtures in full swing I couldn't see too much opening up for me, but that night I got a surprise phone call from David Kohler.

"Lennie, Sam Hammam wants to talk to you," he told me. "I've given him your number, so expect a call."

14

BOSS

After finishing my conversation with David I didn't have to wait too long before the phone rang again, and this time there was no mistaking the enthusiastic sound of Sam Hammam's voice.

"Boss, boss, we need to have a meeting," he said. Sam always used the term 'boss' when he talked to me and I think he did the same with pretty much everyone he spoke to. He'd earned a reputation as one of the game's characters during his time as chairman of Wimbledon, and since selling the club he'd moved on to Cardiff City and was now in charge of them, with former Wimbledon player, Alan Cork, as their manager.

"Come to my house on Sunday," Sam added urgently.

I told him that I'd just arranged to go away for a few days with Jenny and have a bit of a break over the New Year period. I suggested that we talked when I got back, but he was keen for us to meet as soon as possible.

"No, no boss," he insisted. "We need you down at Cardiff, I want to talk to you quickly."

In the end we agreed to meet at the Landmark Hotel in Marylebone the next night, and at 10am on Sunday morning I was sitting next to him in his car heading for Cardiff. The job Sam wanted to offer me was director of football at the club, with Corky remaining as manager. So in a crazy 48 hour period I had been sacked on the Friday morning, interviewed and offered a job the following night, and appointed as Cardiff City's director of football on the Sunday!

Lennie

I met Alan Cork on that Sunday and stayed around the next day just to sort a few things out. Cardiff had spent a lot of money since Sam had become their owner, and in the previous season they'd won promotion from Division Three. It was obvious that Sam wanted success quickly at the club, and it was also very clear that Cardiff City had the fan base and potential to one day compete right at the top. Having gained promotion at the end of the previous season, I think the plan was to go straight through Division One and continue the climb.

A week after I was appointed they were due to play at home in the FA Cup third round against Leeds, who were going great guns and were reckoned to be one of the top sides in the country. Leeds had a home league game against West Ham on New Year's Day and I wanted to go to the match and check them out before the Cup clash, but I almost didn't make it back.

I went to the Leeds game and they were awesome beating West Ham 3-0 to go top of the Premiership. I'd decided that it would make sense for me to drop off at my rented bungalow as part of the trip so that I could pick up some more of my things, because I would have to relocate once again now I'd been given the Cardiff job. The weather was terrible as I drove back, particularly in the rural areas near to the bungalow. I'm not sure how it happened but as I took a bend in a country road I suddenly lost control of the Mercedes I was driving and it turned over coming to a halt in a field. I was on my side in the car, but luckily I quickly realised I wasn't hurt and was able to push the passenger door open and climb out through it, unhurt and unharmed. The car stood up to the impact of it and I eventually continued my journey back to Cardiff, where I was due to attend a press conference.

That wasn't the only time I had problems with my car soon after joining Cardiff, although the next time it was a problem of my own making.

One evening I was on my way home from the ground and stopped at a newsagents to buy a paper. When I came out my car was gone, not only that but I'd left my briefcase and credit cards in it and there was no sign of them either. I'd been in the shop for a matter of minutes, but stupidly I'd left the car engine running while I nipped in. It was something I'd done for years and never had any trouble, but on this occasion it caused me all sorts of hassle. I had to cancel all of my cards, and then there was the problem of having my car nicked. A couple of days later someone from the club saw it being driven by joy riders near the ground and actually tried to chase after them. They didn't manage to get the car back, but happily not long after that it turned up and I gratefully took it back vowing never to jump out and leave the engine running ever again.

The announcement about my new role at the club was made a couple of days before the Leeds match and the press conference was really all about the massive game that was coming up in the Cup. It gave me a taste of just how big a club Cardiff were. They may have been playing their football two divisions below Leeds, but I soon realised that in terms of media coverage, Cardiff were huge and were constantly under the spotlight.

I think Sam's arrival had given the club and its fans new hope that they could finally pull themselves away from the lower reaches of the game, and begin to think about mixing it with the big boys. Playing Leeds was a perfect game for Sam and the club to show the progress that had been made. There had been a bit of pre-match friction created when the Leeds manager, David O'Leary, had asked for the tie to be switched to the Millennium Stadium. He'd also made some comment about Leeds being capable of starting and finishing their Cup campaign in Cardiff because, of course, the Millennium was being used for the FA Cup final at that time, while the new Wembley was under construction. Sam was never slow in seizing an opportunity to get publicity for his club and to wind the opposition up if he could, and had said that Cardiff were a bigger club than Leeds. It just added to the electric atmosphere that was created by the match with 22,000 packed into Ninian Park on the day.

I was really only a spectator at the game, but I did have a quick chat with Alan Cork before the kick-off about the tactics he was going to use, and they seemed very sound against a team who I had been deeply impressed by five days earlier in that West Ham game. I took my seat in the director's box alongside Sam and soon realised what an intimidating place Ninian Park was, the crowd were really passionate and everyone was up for the game. Leeds took an early lead through Mark Viduka but then Graham Kavanagh, who had played for me at Middlesbrough equalised. They had Alan Smith sent off and Sam increased the emotions by leaving the director's box and walking around the edge of the pitch while play was still going on. It was something I'd seen him do in his Wimbledon days, but it never quite had the same effect as it did on this particular day. It led to quite a bit of trouble in the stands and police had to wade in with dogs to try and restore order. It was that sort of day.

Just to cap it all, Cardiff scored through Scott Young with three minutes remaining to claim a famous victory. It was a bitter pill for Leeds to have to swallow and nobody felt it more than David O'Leary. Sam was delighted with what had happened and couldn't help having one more little pop as the Leeds team left the ground. He shouted out reminding them what he'd said about Cardiff being the bigger club, and also saying that their Cup run had started and ended in Cardiff. It was all too much for David and he ended up grabbing a startled Sam by the lapels of his jacket, before the incident was broken up. It was all quite an introduction to my new club.

After that game I was able to get stuck into the job I'd been brought to the club to do. Basically I had a brief to look at all aspects of Cardiff from top to bottom and used my experience in the areas where I could help and improve things. Alan Cork was the manager of the club and he had his staff and got on with things in the way that he saw fit. I was there to help him in any way I could, but there was no way I was going to interfere while he was running the team because that was his job and I knew just how tough it could be. If he wanted to discuss things with me or run something past me I was there. I was also happy to give any advice if he asked for it. I got on well with Corky and still do, but I also got the impression that his relationship with Sam, which had started way back in their Wimbledon days, had started to fray at the edges a bit.

The results weren't bad at all with four wins out of the next six league games leaving the team eighth in the table, but then came a five day period which changed matters dramatically. We went to London for a midweek game against a Brentford side that were managed by Steve Coppell. We were 1-0 up at the break, but then Steve changed things around at half-time and Brentford were a different outfit, scoring twice and ending the game as 2-1 winners. On the Saturday following that match we went to Wigan, who were in the lower half of the table, and it finished 4-0 to them, a comprehensive battering.

The crowd were getting on to Corky and on the way home to Cardiff I had a conversation with him, which was all about the situation he found himself in and what he wanted to do about it. I was honest and up front telling him that if he wanted to carry on we would support him, but at the same time I said that if the team didn't start to win then he could expect things to get a bit hairy and it would probably get decidedly unpleasant. I had watched him and thought that a lot of the criticism he was receiving was starting to get to him. It was a shame but I'd been in the game long enough to recognise the signs. I told him to have a good old think about everything and said that if he wanted to call it a day, the club would understand and make sure that he was properly looked after when it came to sorting out his contract.

It was one of those moments that most managers face at some time in their career, when it's pretty obvious your time is up. If you stay around too long after that happens then it can leave you as an absolute wreck. Sometimes the bravest decision is to just end it and walk away from a club, because it's the best thing for everyone concerned. If you stay, all you're really doing is prolonging the agony and it can have an on-going affect on the rest of your career. At no time did I or the club force Corky to leave, but when he made the decision to go I think it was the right one for him at that time.

So he went and I was asked to take over as manager. I'd just had the worst spell I could remember with that sequence of results before I left Grimsby, and what I could not have known when I took over from Corky, was that I was about to experience just about the best spell I'd ever had!

We scratched wins in my first two games in charge which were at home against Bury and Cambridge. Then I decided to change things a little with the way the team played. I used a back four, with a narrow three man midfield and then one striker behind two more at the front. It suited the players I had to work with and, if I say so myself, it worked like a dream. We just sailed on and on with 10 wins and three draws in an unbeaten run which took us to the end of the season. We finished in fourth place, but that was because we ran out of games to play. If there had been another couple of league matches, I'm convinced we would have got automatic promotion, as it was we had to settle for the play-offs, but everyone at the club was very confident we could go all the way and get promotion. We were very strong and were the form team of the division, there was no reason for us to fear anything as we prepared for the first leg of the semi-final against Stoke away.

They had finished one place and three points below us in the table and we knew it would mean two tough games, but they were games which I was confident would see us come out on top. I've never lost a play-off final, but I had lost at the semi-final stage with Luton, which had been a disappointment, and I was about to experience even greater disappointment with what was about to happen against Stoke.

When we arrived at the Britannia Stadium for the first leg I don't think I'd ever seen so many policemen drafted in for a football match before. They seemed to be everywhere, and the atmosphere was electric. We played well and after only 12 minutes Robert Earnshaw gave us the lead, which was the perfect way to start such an important match. With just under an hour of the game gone Leo Fortune-West got our second and the odds of going through to the final looked very much in our favour. It still looked good for us even after Deon Burton, who was on loan from Derby, pulled one back for Stoke with six minutes to go.

We were due to meet for the second leg just three days later on 1st May, and on the day before the game we didn't just have an April shower in Cardiff, we had a full-blown deluge, which restricted our training, but we looked sharp enough the next night when we played the second leg in front of 19,367 people at an excited Ninian Park. There was a lot of expectation on us because we were favourites to go through, not just because we looked stronger on paper, but because we'd managed to come back with a vital first leg win. My experience told me that it was likely to be a very tight affair and that's the way it turned out, but it still looked as though we would get through as the game entered its final moments with the score at 0-0.

Soon after my first two games in charge and before I changed the system, I'd gone back to one of my old clubs and signed a forward named Andy Campbell from Middlesbrough. He'd had a real impact, scoring six goals in his loan spell and we decided to sign him on a permanent deal for £950,000. He got another goal for us soon after the transfer, but then got injured. Robert Earnshaw had been plagued with some injury problems and not been in the side, but when Andy got sidelined it was a chance for Robert to come back in and he'd done a good job, including getting the goal in the first leg against Stoke.

With the clock ticking away in the second leg and with the game goalless, I decided to make a change and bring on Campbell for Earnshaw just to help wind things down. Andy came on and as Stoke passed the ball around they suddenly switched play and the ball went through Campbell's legs. If it had hit his heal or foot it would probably have spun off somewhere and the move might have broken down. Instead they retained possession and their move eventually led to James O'Connor scoring for them in the very last minute of the game. The aggregate score was level and we had to go to extra-time.

After going so close the players had to pick themselves up and make sure they didn't let it all slip away from them. They had done really well since I took over and now they were staring at 30 minutes of football that would have a huge effect on their careers. We created chances but couldn't score and then with five minutes remaining of extra-time, Stoke were awarded a free-kick. They placed the ball and one of their substitutes, Souleymane Oulare, took the kick. Our wall jumped, the ball hit Spencer Prior and deflected into the net. Game over.

It was a really painful experience after all that had happened and the way we'd finished the season. We'd been overwhelming favourites, but we'd lost and it was a loss which I believe proved very costly. We had looked like a runaway train towards the end of the season, with real momentum and it seemed as though nothing was going to stop us getting a promotion place, but the train had been derailed. It was going to be my job to make sure we got back on the right track very quickly.

15

JOINING THE CLUB

Stoke went on to beat Brentford easily in the final, as I believe we would have done. That's no disrespect to Steve Coppell who did a brilliant job for Brentford with very limited resources. It was just that we were a very strong side at the time, with great momentum, but it wasn't to be.

The one thing we couldn't afford to do was dwell on the disappointment, because it was imperative that we didn't lose momentum completely. There was a job to be done and I knew that Sam was desperate to see the club move up the leagues as quickly as possible. I also knew that the coming season was going to be a tough one because there were some very good teams in the league, and it all looked a lot stronger than it had in the season which had just finished.

Happily we got off to a very good start, losing only one of our first 13 league games, so by the time we beat Wycombe 1-0 at home on 12th October, we were at the top of the league. Robert Earnshaw was on fire and scored nine goals during the run, becoming a real favourite with the fans. It looked as though we were good enough to push for promotion, but I realised that it was a long old season and teams like Wigan, Crewe, QPR, Oldham and Bristol City, all looked likely to figure in the shake-up, because they were very strong and competitive.

At the end of November we had to go to Loftus Road to play Rangers who were sixth in the league. We came away with a 4-0 win, with a hat-trick from Earnshaw and another goal from Campbell. Rangers manager Ian Holloway had done a good job with the team, but when we met them they hadn't won for six games, and I think some of their fans were having a bit of a go. In fact, one woman actually jumped out of the crowd and threw her season ticket at Ollie, but in my book you haven't done it as a manager until someone has thrown a ticket in your face! It happened to me in my last season with Middlesbrough. After the game I spoke to one of their directors, Nick Blackburn and the TV commentator, John Motson. I said what a good young manager I thought Ian Holloway was. I don't know if he was under any pressure there at that stage or whether my comments were taken on board by Nick, but Rangers stuck with him and they were rewarded with a tremendous second half to their season.

It was a great result against Rangers who I knew would be up there at the end of the season, I also knew that we faced another test two weeks later when we were due to entertain Bristol City. It was a big game for the team and our fans, but on a personal level it was also a big game for me. I had reached a stage in my career where I'd managed to clock up a managerial milestone by joining a very exclusive club.

Everyone knows that being a manager is a pretty precarious profession. You go into it knowing that it is almost inevitable you will be sacked during your career, not just once, but quite often several times. It was never an easy job, and it's probably got harder in more recent times because of the need to produce almost instant success with the team you're in charge of. If it doesn't happen quickly, then you can be out on your ear and despite what a lot of people may think, there isn't a constant merry-go-round whereby you lose one job and quickly pick up another. The number of managers and coaches who lose their jobs and then are lost to the professional game forever is absolutely staggering. So when you manage to clock up 1,000 competitive matches in English League football, it really is a feat.

That's what happened to me in that game against Bristol City and it meant I was able to join a very select group, alongside Sir Alex Ferguson, Sir Bobby Robson, Sir Matt Busby, Dave Bassett, Alan Buckley, Brian Clough, Dario Gradi, Brian Horton, Harry Redknapp, Joe Royle, Denis Smith, Jim Smith, Alec Stock, Graham Taylor and Neil Warnock. More recently Steve Coppell also joined the club when he reached the mark while managing Reading in 2009.

I was proud to reach the 1,000 game mark and it was difficult to think that I had got my first taste of management 24 years earlier when I took over as caretaker at Plymouth after Mike Kelly had left the club and before Malcolm Allison's arrival. I'd experienced an awful lot since then and despite having to cope with some extremely tough and difficult situations, I also realised that I'd been fortunate to stay in the game on a virtually continuous basis for so long. I actually had a touchline ban for the game against Bristol, only the second time in my career that it had happened. There was a nice meal laid on for me, which Sam turned up late for, but then he gave a speech saying that I would go on to reach the 1,500 game mark.

The only disappointment that day was the result. We lost 2-0 and slipped down to third place in the table, but our form overall from then on was pretty good. Certainly good enough to make sure we stayed in the top four, but unlike the previous season when we'd looked so good towards the end of the season, this time round we started to splutter a little.

We had good wins against Wycombe and Chesterfield in April, but then hit a bad patch at a crucial time in the season and couldn't win any of our final five games. In fact, we lost three in a row and then picked up draws with Wigan and Crewe to eventually limp over the line in sixth place, a point ahead of Tranmere. Wigan romped away with the league finishing top with 100 points and Crewe got the second automatic spot.

We were left with having to face the play-offs again and our opponents in the semi-final were Bristol City.

They had finished third and because of that they had their home game in the second leg. I knew they fancied their chances against us. Not only had they beaten us in that game at Ninian Park in December, but they also repeated the scoreline when they played us in the third from last match of the league season. I have to admit it had been troubling to see the way we'd faded away at the end of the season, but at the same time, experience taught me that the play-offs can be a very different ball game when they get going and matches don't always run true to form. Just look at what happened to us a year earlier.

I was also aware that Sam was very eager for success and having missed out 12 months ago, I knew there was no way he wanted the same thing to happen again. I may have been at the club for less than 18 months, but I got the distinct impression that it was the last chance saloon as far as I was concerned, and I had to get the team up.

City had a little Scottish wide man named Scott Murray, who was very good and had caused problems for us in both the league games we'd played against them. I decided to change the team a bit in order to help us cope with him. It worked well in the first leg which was a tight affair that was settled with 16 minutes to go when Willie Boland crossed the ball and Peter Thorne scored with a header to give us a narrow lead to take into the second leg three days later.

Despite starting the game a goal down I knew they still thought they could turn things around in front of their own fans. They really came at us, particularly after the break, when we couldn't seem to get out of our own half. Danny Gabbidon was immense for us at the back and the only two clear cut chances they managed to create were missed. We defended for our lives, but didn't really create anything. When the final whistle blew the game was still goalless, which meant that unlike the previous year, we had got ourselves into the final. It was a huge relief to get through after all the disappointment of the previous year, but once all the elation had subsided, it didn't take too long for it to dawn on everyone that we still had a huge task in front of us if we were going to get the promotion everyone so desperately wanted.

The great thing was that we knew the final was going to be at the Millennium Stadium. We'd effectively be playing in our own backyard, which was tremendous for the club and for the fans, but at the same time it put massive pressure on us to deliver. Our opponents were going to be Ian Holloway's QPR, who had finished fourth in the league and then knocked out Oldham in their semi-final.

We stayed at The Vale Hotel a lovely place that was probably only about five miles from the stadium where lots of the eventual play-off winners seemed to stay. When we got to within about two miles of the Millennium the team bus could hardly move. The roads and pavements were jam packed with our fans. There were literally thousands of supporters all making their way to the ground. It was a magnificent sight. I later spoke to people who had first gone to Ninian Park and then walked to the Millennium from there. They all said what a deeply moving and emotional experience it was for them, which showed just how much it meant to the supporters and how important it was for the club. It has to be said that the game itself was not a classic, instead it was a very tight affair and with about 10 minutes of the match remaining it was 0-0.

Robert Earnshaw's goal scoring exploits were no flash in the pan. He continued to knock them in and scored 35 goals that season, 31 of them in the league, which was a tremendous contribution to the cause. He had rightly become a big favourite with the fans, so you can imagine their reaction that day when I decided to replace Robert with Andy Campbell as the game headed towards extra-time. It was as if there was a massive intake of breath from the whole stadium. Andy had been injured in the second half of the season and missed quite a few matches, but he came back right at the end of the campaign, and was a good player to have on the bench ready to come on. I felt we just weren't doing enough going forward, even though we didn't really look as though we were going to concede. Most people probably thought I was mad to take off our top goal scorer when we needed a goal, but I had to be brave. Managers have to do that. If you think it's the right thing to do, you have to do it and be broad shouldered enough to take stick if it comes your way. You are paid to make decisions, and I made a big one that day.

The game went into extra-time and there was still nothing to choose between the two sides. With six minutes to go Gareth Whalley stuck a ball over the top. Danny Shittu, the Rangers centre-half, had a split second to decide whether he should cut Campbell in half, ending the danger but probably getting sent off as a consequence. He decided not to, and instead Andy was able to get in and score what proved to be the winning it seemed goal. The stadium erupted. There were 66,000 people in there that day and it seemed like about 40,000 of them were Cardiff supporters. The noise was unbelievable and so were the scenes of pure joy and relief that greeted the final whistle.

At the end of the game after all the presentations I went onto the pitch and Sam came over to me beaming from ear to ear.

"Boss," he shouted at me over all the noise from the crowd. "You've made a whole nation happy!"

I thought it was an interesting comment and I knew what he was saying, not only were the fans delighted to see their team get promotion, they were also proud. Cardiff had seen some dark times in recent years and now the fans and the city had a team who were giving them something to shout about. It felt good to be a part of it and I got a real sense of what it meant to all the supporters when I finally left the ground that day.

My partner, Jenny, actually worked for QPR and was in charge of their ticket office. It caused a bit of a dilemma, because she couldn't really sit with the official party from Cardiff City and she couldn't really sit with her QPR colleagues. In the end I had to get a box at the Millennium and she watched the game from it along with a few of our friends. To be fair to Rangers, they did a very good job of protecting Jenny from the media, because a few of the press boys got wind of the fact that she worked for QPR and lived with the manager of Cardiff. It would obviously have made a good little story, but they batted all enquiries away and it made her life a lot easier during the run-up to the match.

After the game I met her and we walked together from the stadium to the hotel where the reception was to be held. It was only about a quarter of a mile, but it took absolutely ages. The streets were full of celebrating Cardiff fans and they all wanted to stop and say hello and well done. It was a great feeling to be walking through so many people knowing you'd made their day by winning a football match. Mind you, I don't think I'd have fancied doing it if we'd lost and the Campbell substitution hadn't come off!

That day and the intensity of it will live with me forever. If you manage one of the big clubs you probably get used to such big occasions on a regular basis, but for the rest of us we probably have about half a dozen times during our career when it happens, and it is a very special feeling. During the course of the whole day I didn't have one drop of alcohol, not even at the reception, because the last thing I wanted was to forget any of it. At the end of the night I was stone cold sober and even drove back to London so that I could be at a friend's party he was having the next day.

Getting promotion in the way that we did was a classic example of the way the play-offs can be so unpredictable. The year before we had gone into them having finished the season in tremendous form and yet had ended up getting knocked out at the semi-final stage. This time our league form at the end of the season had been decidedly indifferent, but we never let a goal in during three games and finished up being promoted.

We'd made it to Division One, but missing out 12 months earlier had cost us. We had a big wage bill already and everything had been geared up for us to go through the leagues quickly. Not getting promotion first time around had stalled things, and I came to the conclusion some time later, that it had a real effect on my time at the club.

16

GREAT EXPECTATIONS

One of the things of paramount importance to Sam was moving the club to a new stadium. He was desperate for it to happen and never missed an opportunity to bang on about it. He even sat in on the post match press conference after we'd beaten QPR at the Millennium, and spoke at great length about his plans.

Sam had a very strong vision when it came to what he wanted for Cardiff City and he was very ambitious. I knew from the very first day I went to the club that he had great expectations, and he wanted me to help him fulfil those expectations. He knew of me from my Charlton days, and thought I was the right person with the right sort of experience to come in and take a good hard look at the club from top to bottom and tell him what I thought. What was right with it and what was wrong with it. He'd invested a lot of time, money and energy in Cardiff and wanted the club to be successful.

I could understand that and was under no illusions about Sam. I knew he was very much a hands-on chairman who would be very demanding. He paid well and he expected results. Working with him was certainly an experience and I knew pretty quickly that I was dealing with someone who had a complex mixture of characteristics. He had a memory like an elephant, he could be absolutely charming, totally ruthless, cunning, and might cut you to pieces, but I liked him and still do.

I respected what he was trying to do at the club but throughout my time at Cardiff I had some massive rows with him. There were many occasions when I had him on the other end of the phone screaming in my ear about something or other.

"It's my money, not the club's, not yours. It's my money," he'd be shouting.

Then about half an hour later he'd call again to apologise. He wanted to be involved in everything, or at least, know what was going on. One of the biggest rows I ever had with him was when I tried to loan one of our 19-year-old kids to a non-league side in Wales and he didn't know about it. He never tried to stop me doing it, but he was upset about the fact that he hadn't been told. On the other hand, he was quite happy for me to do deals in the transfer market.

I have always dealt with transfers for all of the clubs I have worked for. My attitude is that if there is a chief executive who can do a better deal for the club, then fair enough, they can get on with it, but that has never happened. When I went to Cardiff I never expected to get involved in transfers because of Sam's reputation. He did a brilliant job at Wimbledon, buying cheap and selling very big. He was tremendously successful at it and I saw no reason why that shouldn't be the case at Cardiff. To my surprise, Sam just let me get on with things. I think he trusted me to do the best deal for the club, which was something I always did. I ended up doing most of the transfers. Sometimes he wanted to be involved in every detail, but other times he stood back a lot more and was happy for me to just keep him informed about what I was doing.

He could get upset about all sorts of things and often it would be over something most people would consider to be trivial. I remember on one occasion being in his office, as I often was, talking about players and the team. Sam sent out for some sandwiches, but when they arrived they had some relish in them. He didn't like his sandwiches with relish. Now most people would have pushed them to one side or asked for something else, not Sam. He summoned the three people who had prepared the sandwiches and gave them a huge dressing down which ended with him saying, "If you ever put relish in my sandwiches again, you'll be sacked!" It was incredible, and I bet a few hours later he was charming their socks off. That was him.

He liked to be on the bench, in the dressing room before games and after a match. He very rarely seemed to go in the opposition's director's box. Once, before a home match, the team were out on the pitch doing their pre-match warm-up, and Sam wandered down to watch. George Wood, who was our goalkeeping coach, was out on the pitch with the team and when he'd finished doing his bit he took a breather in the dug-out. Music was playing in the background on the public address system and one of the songs that came on was the famous *Three Lions* tune that England had used as an anthem during the Euro '96 Championships. George started singing along to the tune and Sam came over and joined him, happily humming away to the record. About half way through the song Sam turned to George and asked him what the song was.

"It's that *Three Lions* song," George informed him. "You know, the one England supporters used to sing in Euro '96."

"What!" shouted Sam.

He promptly went to see the guy who used to play all the records at the ground and sacked him on the spot for playing a song that was so closely associated with the England team, five minutes earlier he'd been humming along to it himself.

Sam could also be very generous and lavish, he once took Jenny and I, together with a Cardiff director named Michael Isaac, to tea at Claridge's followed by the ballet *Swan Lake* and then finally dinner at The Ivy. I have to admit it was all a little bit wasted on me, but nevertheless it was a marvellous experience and a very nice gesture.

He seemed happier mixing with the players and, of course, the fans. I've already mentioned the incident during the Leeds game when he walked around the edge of the pitch. That caused mayhem and the authorities were quick to stop him doing that sort of thing again, but the Cardiff fans loved it and from my very first day at the club it was clear he had a real affinity with the supporters.

On my first night he insisted on picking me up at my hotel and going to dinner before going on to introduce me to some of the hard core supporters in the city. He loved them and they loved him. There was a real rapport between them and it was hard to think of any other chairman who would have done the same thing. It also gave me an instant understanding of what he was trying to do and what he was promising the supporters. He'd whipped the place up into a frenzy of expectation and everyone expected him to deliver.

Sam never thought small it was always big and the fans responded to that. They'd been in the football doldrums for too long. Sam had come along and bought their club promising to make it a huge force. He would often say to me that he didn't care about the Premiership. It was the Champions League that interested him. During the previous season when we were going great guns in the league, we were drawn away to Tottenham in the Worthington Cup. We lost the game 1-0, but afterwards Sam could be heard telling anyone who was listening just what he expected to happen in the future.

"In 10 years you'll be a feeder club for us!" he said, and he wasn't joking.

To be fair to Sam, although Cardiff were in Division Two when I joined them, I soon came to realise that in so many ways they had a lot in common with a Premier League outfit. In terms of size, potential and media interest, they were very much like a Premier League side. He was a football man and knew the game and the players and people involved, he also understood the demands of my job.

"You do well, boss," he told me once. "You've got to train the players, manage the players and manage me!"

I never really knew when Sam would turn up either, which I think he quite liked. I very quickly got myself an apartment in Cardiff, because I knew it was essential that I was there on a day-to-day basis, and the job was too big for me to live miles away. Sam never actually lived in Cardiff. He would spend two or three days in London and then phone and say he was driving to Cardiff. He'd stay in a hotel for one, two or maybe three days and then be off. He'd also often say he was coming and give me a set time for his arrival, but then not turn up at all. Whether he was physically there or not, you couldn't escape his presence at the club. He had everyone on their toes and ran it very much as his club.

He knew just how demanding he could be, but that didn't mean he was ever going to pull back, and having got promotion it was now full steam ahead to try and get out of the division as soon as possible and get into the Premiership, but trying to get successive promotions is a very difficult thing to achieve.

Having got promotion through the play-offs our season had stretched into late May, but I was determined to try and unwind with a decent holiday. In reality what happened was that I spent most of my time walking up and down a Spanish beach with my mobile phone pressed up against my ear talking to Sam. I shouldn't have expected anything less.

We started well enough and by the start of September a 5-0 home win against Gillingham saw us jump into sixth place in the league. We played some attractive football and Earnshaw once again showed that he could score goals. It all looked very promising, but we hit a bit of a wall in December and couldn't win for five games, slipping from a very respectable seventh in the table to end the year in 12th place. It was still pretty good for a promoted team, but the expectation levels had gone up a notch or two with both Sam, and the fans, wanting us to maintain the success we'd had in the previous season.

Things didn't improve in the New Year and we fell away a bit. There was never any question of us being threatened by the thought of relegation, but at the same time we struggled to find any sort of consistent form and the prospect of another promotion was never a reality as we finally finished the season in 13th position. It was respectable enough for a team that had been promoted, but it wasn't spectacular. I knew Sam didn't want to hang around in a league that underwent a change of name in the summer of 2004 and became the Championship. I also knew there would be pressure on to make a push for promotion when the 2004-05 season began. I added to the squad by bringing in Robert Page, Tony Warner and Jobi McAnuff, but we made a dreadful start winning once in the first nine league games, and very quickly found ourselves in an early season scrap at the bottom. We were struggling on the pitch, and I soon became aware that we were struggling off it as well.

Perhaps one of the first signs for me came with the transfer of Robert Earnshaw to Premiership new boys, West Bromwich Albion, soon after the season started. Robert had done really well for me during my time at the club, and his goal scoring had made him a firm favourite with the fans, but Albion were prepared to pay £3 million for him, and it was clearly the sort of money Cardiff could not turn down. The deal was done at the end of August, just before the transfer window was due to close, in the early hours of the morning after we had lost 2-1 at Wigan. It was a frantic affair that eventually saw Earnshaw being rushed to the home of West Brom secretary, Dr John Evans, signing at about two in the morning.

It was a big fee and it was structured so that Cardiff would get £1 million straight away, £1 million 12 months later, and then the final £1 million a year after that. However, there was a way of getting virtually the whole amount all at once, and that was to go to one of the financial institutions and 'discount' the money. In other words for a fee of say £150,000, they would give you the other £2 million there and then, rather than waiting for the instalment payments. I'd done this before at other clubs, and although, in effect, you weren't going to get the full amount of the transfer because of the discounting fee, it was still a good way to make sure you got a lot of cash into a club all at once.

Losing Earnshaw and his goals was a blow to us, particularly as our start had been so poor. If I'm honest I have to say that at the time I had a big workload. In many ways it was three jobs. I was still fulfilling the director of football role, I was the team manager and I was doing a lot of the coaching alongside my assistant Ian Butterworth. With only a couple of league wins in our first dozen games Sam was naturally concerned. He'd wanted things to happen quickly and having promised such great things, he clearly didn't fancy the prospect of a possible relegation battle. He'd said to me on several occasions that he thought bringing in Terry Burton would be a real help to me, I agreed but didn't think he'd be able to get him to come to the club. Terry was an excellent coach and respected throughout the game as one of the best in the business. At the time he was assistant manager to Ray Lewington at Watford, but Sam knew Terry well from their days at Wimbledon together and was confident he would get his man, which was exactly what he did.

Terry came and worked alongside me while Ian Butterworth left the club. I also had one of my old players, Paul Wilkinson, at the club working as reserve team coach. I knew of Terry but didn't know him that well as a person. It could have been an awkward situation for both of us, being thrown together in difficult circumstances, but I can honestly say that we got on like a house on fire and I could soon see what a top notch coach he was. Sam also made another change bringing in physio Steve Allen, who had also been at Wimbledon. In fact, I had an outstanding staff at the club and we all worked well together. That also applied to other people at the club, like secretary, Jason Turner, who was superb at his job and I worked closely with him. He was a great help to me throughout my time at Ninian Park, just as Luton's secretary, Cherry Newbery, had been when I was at Kenilworth Road.

One other person who was in the background, but had a massively important role in the story of Cardiff City at that time was Michael Isaac. He was nothing like Sam in the way he went about things, and just seemed happy to keep a low profile and do all he could to help the club he loved.

I have to say that the first half of the season was a real struggle and we had a spell between the middle of October and the end of the year, where we only won a couple of league games. We drew quite a few, but that wasn't going to get us away from the wrong end of the table. Not surprisingly the natives started to get restless, as any supporters would do. There had been a lot of promise at the start of the previous season, when the team produced some very good football, the best for years according to many people who had watched Cardiff for a long time. Unfortunately, that promise disappeared in the second half of the season, and as so often happens, the poor form carried on into the start of the next campaign. I believe that is the case four times out of five, unless there is radical change at a club during the summer period. The bad form is carried over and there was certainly evidence of that in our case.

Things started to pick up for us at the beginning of the year and we were unbeaten in the league through January, winning three games and drawing the other, 13 points that were invaluable to us, but we still found ourselves down the bottom in 21st place.

It wasn't a great position to be in and there is inevitable pressure, but

I had been in the game a long time and that experience coupled with the sort of personality I have, seemed to help me cope. I'd be lying if I said it wasn't draining, and off the pitch I was soon dealing with the sort of financial issues most managers never have to get involved in.

The Earnshaw transfer probably signalled the fact that the club wanted to get some much needed money in. It was a very big fee, but by the turn of the year it became obvious that there were still problems with money. The club apparently had debts of around £30 million and Sam was in contact with the former Leeds chairman, Peter Ridsdale, who eventually came to the club to try and help sort out the financial problems. Pretty soon it began to get messy and I found myself having to spend a lot of time and energy in trying to secure a loan from the Professional Footballers Association, because at one stage it looked as though the players were not going to be paid.

It happened in March 2005 and I have to say it was a highly complex thing to have to deal with and very difficult to actually nail down, but I managed to do it, working with our chief executive, David Temme, Jason, and Mick McGuire from the PFA, who was very helpful throughout. We managed to secure a loan of £250,000 to keep things ticking over, but it was very complicated, very time consuming and a long protracted business. It's a high skill but at least I could call on my experience with all the financial difficulties we had at Charlton, and the thing got done.

Although Sam was the owner of the club and had a big shareholding in it, Michael Isaac was, and still is, an extremely successful and wealthy businessman. He had put a substantial amount of his own money into Cardiff and helped the club enormously. As I tried to make sure the players were paid, I went to him to see if he would cover the wage bill. Michael said he'd reached a point where he felt enough was enough, and being the straight sort of person he is, decided to let Terry and I know face to face just why he wasn't prepared to carry on pumping cash in. There were all sorts of stories in the papers about the cash crisis at the club and along with it all the obvious conjecture about which players were going to be sold and when.

At the beginning of March there was another indication of just how tough things were when I had to sell Graham Kavanagh. He was a huge favourite with the fans and never could a Dublin born Irishman have been so popular in Wales. In many ways he was viewed as Mr Cardiff City. He loved the club and played his heart out whenever he pulled on a blue shirt. Kav probably thought he was going to be at Cardiff for the rest of his life, but Paul Jewell, the Wigan manager fancied him as a player and someone who could help them, not just that season, but also in the next because they were pushing for automatic promotion. They also knew we were up against it financially. Graham didn't really want to leave but they offered £600,000 and we pretty much bit their hand off. They were very keen on him and even sent a helicopter down to take him back so that he could sign in time to play against fellow promotion hopefuls Ipswich that weekend. They won that game and finished second in the league getting promotion, while Ipswich ended up third and were knocked out by West Ham in the play-offs. Kav played in every game for Wigan until the end of the season and then went on to have a great career with them in the Premiership. We got the cash the club needed and once again I had to go through the process of discounting it to make sure we got it all up front.

I also had to face a grilling from the press a couple of days later following our 1-0 home win against Sheffield United, which was fair enough. They had their jobs to do and Cardiff City's financial crisis occupied an awful lot of column inches. I think they respected the fact that whatever was happening I was doing my best for the club both on the pitch and off of it. I later heard from Michael Isaac that Sam actually said to him at one stage that I was more than a manager, I was running the club like a director, and I suppose in a way that was what was happening. I was certainly wearing more than just one hat, but I didn't mind that. I'd had to deal with footballing and non-footballing problems throughout my career, this was just another twist. I was getting some stick and so was Sam, with some fans very upset with what was happening after all the very bullish talk when he first took over the club. I just got on with it.

Peter Ridsdale came in as a consultant at the beginning of April and I got on fine with him. One of the things he said to me as soon as he arrived was, "Please keep us in the league." I knew it was imperative that happened if the club were ever going to get out of their financial problems and move forward. At the time we were in 21st place in the table and there were still people who thought we were for the drop, but two wins and two draws from our last four games saw us safe finishing in 16th place. Considering all that had happened and all that was still going on, I considered it a job well done. Certainly what I'd had to do during the last six months or so of the season was way above and beyond the call of duty.

The rumbling of discontent from some supporters was still there as was the speculation surrounding my own position, but I genuinely felt I'd done enough to at least be given a good crack at it when the new season began. If things still didn't pick up on the pitch by that time, I knew what was likely to happen. The axe would fall and I'd be looking for a new job.

17

RETURN WITH ROVERS

When the axe did fall it was the timing of it which surprised me. When the season came to an end I went off to do part of my pro-licence coaching badge, which involved going on a study visit abroad. Basically it meant that I had to visit a club, study their methods and then do a report on my observations and conclusions. I told Sam that I was off to Norway for three days, because I'd decided to take a look at Viking Stavanger, a team that was being managed by Roy Hodgson. I had a feeling before I went that Sam wasn't exactly sure what he wanted to do about me, but I still thought I might get the chance to at least start the new season.

I flew out to Norway with Paul Wilkinson and Geraint Williams, who at that time was assistant manager to Phil Parkinson at Colchester. It was a three day trip and while I was there I received a phone call from a local press guy in Cardiff to say that Sam had been seen talking to the former Wolves manager Dave Jones in the Landmark Hotel in London. The same hotel I'd met Sam when he asked me to become Cardiff's director of football and a place that I knew he used all the time for various business meetings.

You didn't have to be a genius to figure out what might be happening and I knew right there and then it was over for me. We flew back on a Monday morning and I had arranged to meet both Sam and Peter Ridsdale at the Landmark. By then it was no surprise to hear what they had to say. They'd decided on a change and that was it. In my experience when things like that happen, there's absolutely no point in making things worse, and the sensible thing is to try and work things out amicably, with both sides then moving on. Sam and Peter wanted to know what I intended to do having been given the news, and so I told them.

"I'm going to drive to Cardiff now," I said. "I'll get my stuff out of the ground tonight when everybody's gone. I'll see some people very early on tomorrow morning, say my goodbyes and then I'm gone."

They seemed pleased at the way I was taking the whole thing and probably a bit relieved that I wasn't going to start going to the press or kicking up a song and dance about everything, but that just isn't my style. A lot of people said to me that they thought it was terrible the way they went behind my back and started talking to Jonesy while I was still in the job, but that's football. If a chairman or the board have decided on a change it makes their life easier if they've already identified the person they want, and are able to have a plan in place already. I don't blame Sam or Peter Ridsdale, and I certainly don't blame Dave Jones. I got on well with him before he became the Cardiff manager, and I still do now.

My time was up. I thought I might have got the start of the following season but I didn't. It wasn't a total surprise that they were thinking about bringing someone else in, it was the timing of it. When it did all end I was tired by it all. I'd been battered for three and a half years. There had been an awful lot involved in the job. For the vast majority of my time there I had to do virtually all the training, I'd had to deal with Sam on a daily basis, deal with the media requirements – it was an exhausting job. It got easier when Terry Burton came, but it was still a very demanding job. Don't get me wrong, I wouldn't have missed it and working for Cardiff was a great experience.

I still believe to this day that not going up in that first season I was there was a real missed opportunity. Everything was geared up for success and the momentum that Sam had started when he first arrived, would have carried on, but instead it stalled for a year and I personally think that was costly on all sorts of levels for the club. But I genuinely felt I had left the club in a better state than I had found it, and I'm proud to have played my part in the history of Cardiff City at what was a very exciting time for everyone concerned with them. I'm also proud of the fact that my transfer dealings show a profit of around £1 million during my time with them, and that along with David Temme and Matthew Crocker, I was instrumental in helping to set up the centre of excellence which has since produced some outstanding young players such as Aaron Ramsey and Chris Gunter. Players who have made money for the club in transfer fees, just like Cameron Jerome, who arrived at Cardiff as a non-contract player on about £125 per week and was sold to Birmingham after I'd left.

I enjoyed my time at Cardiff as tough as it could be on occasions, and as I've said I still like Sam and bear no grudges at all. Getting jobs and getting the sack is all part of football life as a manager and as I headed out of Wales on that Tuesday morning I realised I was back in the job market again. I had never been the sort of person to sit back and wait for things to happen, and I knew that if I wanted to start the season with a new club I had to begin looking pretty quickly.

The summer is quite often the time when there are managerial changes, following the ending of one season and the preparation for a new one. That summer Millwall were looking for a new manager after Dennis Wise had left the club. They also had a new chairman after Theo Paphitis stepped down. Jeff Burnige took over and started the search for someone to replace Wisey.

It all happened very soon after I'd parted company with Cardiff and I was still finishing off my pro-licence in Wales. I got a call to ask me to meet Jeff Burnige in London and spent two hours with him finding out exactly what he wanted from a new manager and what was going to happen at the club. The interview went well and I felt pretty confident of getting the job, I also felt it was something I could do well and that Burnige seemed to think I was the right sort of person for them at that time. It sounded as though there were a lot of things that needed to be sorted out.

Nothing happened for a few days and then I began to see stories linking Millwall with George Burley, who had just left Derby. George had earned a reputation as a good young manager, whose career was very much in the ascendancy, but with all due respect to Millwall, I just couldn't see him wanting to go there. In the end, despite the speculation, Burley didn't take over at Millwall, but I kind of think that being linked with him put the club off the scent a little bit. They seemed to change their mind about the sort of manager they wanted and rather than go for someone with my background and experience, they decided to give the job to Steve Claridge, who had played for the club and had a brief period in charge at Portsmouth. It didn't quite turn out as Steve or Jeff must have hoped, because Jeff resigned as chairman after a couple of months in control, and Steve found himself out of the job after just 36 days in charge.

Some years later I saw Jeff at a reserve team game and he told me he should have given me the job. Kenny Jackett, who was the Swansea manager at the time, also thought I should have got the job and was surprised I didn't. Millwall struggled getting relegated in 2006 and after three more managers following Steve Claridge's departure, they appointed Kenny to the job in 2007. He had done a great job with Swansea and I believe he's a very good manager. Millwall look like a different outfit since he took over and they came extremely close to getting promoted to the Championship in 2009. I felt a bit unlucky at missing out on Millwall back then and it meant I was still on the look-out for a job. I had the feeling that if George Burley's name hadn't come up in connection with it,

I would probably have got the job. Without being conceited, on previous occasions whenever I'd got to the interview stage, I'd ended up getting the job, so this was a new experience for me. I just had to carry on putting myself in the frame for anything else that I liked the look of and not too long afterwards one of my old clubs were in need of a new manager when Bobby Williamson left Plymouth.

It had been 28 years since I first went to Home Park to work with Mike Kelly, and more than 27 years since I had that brief stint in charge as manager before Malcolm Allison's arrival. I fancied the idea of going back there and as a Championship team, Plymouth were in a division I knew all about and was keen to work in again. I got myself an interview on a list of about six candidates, one of whom was Tony Pulis. He was at Stoke but the story was that provided everything could be agreed between the two clubs, Tony was the favourite to become the new man at Plymouth. In the local press at the time the story was that it was between me and him and it ended with me, in effect, being the runner-up again when he was appointed as their new manager.

The third opportunity that summer came after the season had already got underway as Bristol City looked for a new manager to replace Brian Tinnion. My name was linked with the job and I went along for an interview, which I again thought went well. I was even asked by them to watch one of their games and I thought I was in with a very good chance of getting the job. But having had the interview and watched the match as they'd asked, I knew that if I was going to get it I'd be hearing from them within a couple of days. Instead, it all went quiet and they appointed Gary Johnson who had done a very good job with Yeovil. In fairness to Gary, he's since done very well at City and has really sorted the place out. I certainly couldn't say I would have done any better, but having left Cardiff four months earlier I was still no nearer to getting another job. It was a new experience for me. It seemed I'd finished runner-up on three separate occasions.

When you've been in for three jobs in a relatively short space of time and not got any of them, you start to think about what has happened and ask yourself questions. Was it just bad luck? Was it my age? Were they looking for a different type of person? Maybe it was just the set of circumstances that came with each job that dictated the eventual outcome? Maybe all the clubs had been looking for someone other than me, but at the same time I was in there as a safe pair of hands if they didn't get the man they wanted? They were all questions that went through my mind at the time, but whatever the reasons I knew I couldn't afford to let it worry me.

I had been on a six-month rolling contract at Cardiff, which meant that in effect that was my period of notice and as such the club had agreed to pay me for six months following my departure. I decided to let the six months period run down and around November time City's Bristol rivals, Rovers, were looking to appoint a director of football, the title I had originally been given by Sam at Cardiff. It was something I fancied the look of, but my biggest decision didn't concern the job it was whether I fancied dropping down to operate in League Two. The last time I'd worked at that level was when I was assistant to Colin Murphy at Lincoln and I had to weigh up the consequences and possibilities.

It was also the sort of job I felt was right for me at the time. I'm not sure I could have done it as a 48-year-old or as a 38-year-old, but at nearly 58, I felt I had the experience and know-how to make the role work. Geoff Dunford was the chairman and I went along for an informal interview with a few of the board, before attending a more formal one a bit later. The club had clearly thought about the way they wanted to go in terms of management structure and had appointed Paul Trollope as team manager a couple of months earlier.

They obviously wanted a new system and they wanted it to succeed having almost dropped out of league football three years earlier when they finished one off the bottom of what was then called Division Three. I think they'd checked me out and talked to people in the game who had said, "If Lennie can't do it, nobody can do it."

After my hat-trick of near misses, it felt good to be back in the game once more.

18

LIFE'S A GAS

The idea of joining Bristol Rovers as their new director of football was really appealing, but I was very much aware that it wasn't all about me. Paul Trollope was the manager and had only been in the job a couple of months. If the whole thing was going to be successful I knew the two of us had to be able to get on and work together.

I'd known Trolls as a player when he'd been in sides that played against teams I was managing, but apart from that we'd never really had the opportunity to talk at any great length. I got the chance to put that right pretty quickly when I met him at a charity dinner in Swindon on a Sunday night in early November 2005, which I went along to with some of the Rovers directors. I sat with Paul and went over a few things with him, and we seemed to get on well enough. We were both keen to make things work and when the official announcement of my appointment was made the next day, we were off and running. I also think the Rovers directors deserved some credit for making a bold decision to try something different and take the club in a new direction.

I'd been given pretty much a blank canvas in terms of the way I went about the job, and I knew that in order to make it work Paul had to be happy with me, and then it was a case of looking at areas where he might need me. One of the biggest things I had going for me was that I've done everything at a club during my time as a coach and manager. Whether it's coaching, tactics, player selection, transfers, scouting, finances or whatever else, I've been there and done it. The only thing I'll hold my hands up to and say I'm lacking in is IT skills, but in real every day terms, I know the game inside out and the thing I wanted to make sure Trolls understood was that I was there to help him.

I realised the situation could potentially be awkward, but I also knew that if we were both determined to make it work, it would. On the day of the first game I was involved in, which was a home match with Rochdale, Paul was interviewed by a local TV guy who asked him whether he knew that when I was director of football at Cardiff, I was manager within weeks and Alan Cork was gone. The clear inference was that Trolls should watch his back because I was after his job, but that simply wasn't the case and neither was it with regard to Corky. The whole Cardiff thing with Alan and Sam was probably something that would have happened whether I was there or not, but when he went they saw me taking over as the obvious move.

Paul had only been in the job for a matter of weeks and we were pretty much starting off together as a new management team. He and I seemed to settle into a pattern pretty quickly and it hasn't really changed to this day. I'm his mentor, assistant, and I help with the coaching, as well as providing a link with the boardroom. I try to steer him through it all, but right from day one it was down to him to make the key decisions. He decides who plays and who gets dropped. I have my say and give him my opinions, but that's as far as it goes. I spent the first six months giving him 'what ifs?' By that I mean I would say to him, "What if this happens? What are you going to do about that? What would you do about this or that situation?" It was my way of trying to prepare him, not just in coaching and team selection, but also for management in general. I could see he was a bright young coach and I also saw my role as making sure that he had a future in the game. Paul was a good coach and wanted a career in management. I wanted to make sure I gave him all the help I could, and in doing so the club would hopefully prosper and benefit.

Part of the pattern we settled into early on was me sitting on the bench with him, which was something he wanted. It worked well from the start. Paul liked to stand in the technical area and I sat there watching and making suggestions. Sometimes I put my opinion forward more forcefully than others, but from day one it had to be a case of him making the final decision. The first season went pretty well, with us both getting to know each other and at the same time getting to know the way we liked to work. We picked up reasonably well in the early part of 2006, getting up as high as eighth in the table at one stage and finished the campaign in 12th place.

The first month of the new season brought some inconsistent results as we won two and lost three of the five league matches we played in August. Looking back now, probably the most significant thing which happened was the arrival of striker Rickie Lambert from Rochdale for £200,000 on transfer deadline day at the end of that month. Junior Agogo had gone to Nottingham Forest for a similar fee a couple of days earlier, and we'd known that he was likely to be leaving. So we drew up a short-list of possible people we would like to bring in and Lambert was on it. When he first arrived he struggled with some injury problems and wasn't really fit for some time, but once he got into his stride, Rickie began to show just what a good player he was, scoring some crucial goals, including a couple which had very significant consequences.

Another significant moment came in mid-October, although at the time nobody at the club could have envisaged what it would lead to. We were drawn at home to Torquay United in the first round of the southern section of the Johnstone's Paint Trophy. A competition for clubs in Leagues One and Two with the final due to take place at the Millennium Stadium the following April. The match was given a little extra spice by the fact that the Torquay manager was Ian Atkins, who had been in charge at Rovers before Paul took over. We won the game 1-0 with a great header from Byron Anthony a minute from time, and then went on to beat Wycombe 2-0 at their place and Peterborough 1-0 at home to reach the semi-final stage, where we were drawn away to Shrewsbury. I know a lot of people will say that on paper the match didn't look as though it would get fans wildly excited, but the fact was that by the time we came to play the game, we knew that if we won we'd be playing Bristol City over two legs in the southern section final, a huge game for each club with the prospect of full houses at both grounds.

We travelled to Shrewsbury to play the game and it was frozen off. The ground was in such a state that we shouldn't have even been there. When we went back to play the match again some time later they reckoned that the pitch was fit to play on, but I told them they were having a laugh, and it got called off again. It was a Tuesday night and on the following Saturday we were due to play at Derby in the fourth round of the FA Cup, having beaten Barrow, Bournemouth and Hereford to get to that stage.

Shrewsbury weren't in the FA Cup having been knocked out by Hereford in the first round, and they didn't have a league game either, so it meant that while we were playing Derby, they would have the weekend off. Quite literally, as we were driving away from the postponed game on that Tuesday night, Shrewsbury were announcing on their website that our game with them was now going to be played on the following Monday.

I'd known their manager, Gary Peters, for a long time and he'd done exactly what I would have done in his shoes. He'd tried to get the game played as quickly as possible knowing that it would give us less recovery time, but when I heard about it I decided that it just wasn't on. It wasn't fair on us and I was determined to make sure we had the best possible chance of going through, because I knew what two huge games against our local rivals would mean, not just to the fans but also to the finances of the club. As director of football at Bristol Rovers I considered it part of my job to make sure I used all my experience, know-how and contacts within the game in the best interests of the club and a situation like this called for swift action. I managed to obtain the mobile number of Andy Williamson, who was the director of operations at the Football League. He was at another match that night but I managed to speak to him during the half-time break and explained the whole thing to him. The outcome of it all was that the game was eventually played on the following Tuesday and not 24 hours earlier as Shrewsbury wanted, we won with the only goal of the match scored by Richard Walker, and set ourselves up for a southern section two-leg final against City.

We played the two games six days apart in February and they were two massive matches for the city of Bristol. The first was in front of a full house at their place on a Wednesday night and we came away with a 0-0 draw. The second game took place on the following Tuesday and our ground was bursting at the seams on the night. We won 1-0 and with a goal from Rickie Lambert, the first of those two very significant goals I mentioned earlier, because this one put us in the final at the Millennium Stadium against Doncaster Rovers on Sunday 1st April.

The crowd figure on the day of the final was 59,024 and 40,000 of them were Rovers supporters, or Gasheads, as they are known throughout the city because the club are often referred to as The Gas, getting the nickname from the fact that Rovers' former Eastville ground was situated near gasworks. It was quite incredible but also an indication of the fan base and potential of the club. I had very happy memories of my last visit to the Stadium with a team because, of course, it was where Cardiff had got that fantastic play-off win against QPR almost three years earlier. It wasn't such a happy outcome for me this time round because we lost the game 3-2 after extra-time. We got off to the worst possible start conceding inside the first minute, when Jonathan Forte scored for them. Ex-Bristol city man, Paul Heffernan put them two up after five minutes to really rock us back, but in the second half we got into the game when Richard Walker scored from the penalty spot and then Sammy Igoe levelled the scores just after the hour forcing extra-time. The winner was scored for them by Graeme Lee 10 minutes from the end of the match. It was disappointing for everyone, but the great thing about it was that the club had made at least £500,000 from the competition, which was a lot of money. We'd also taken in some cash from the run we'd had in the FA Cup, and although that had come to an end at Derby when Paul Peschisolido scored for them eight minutes from time, getting to the fourth round had still been very good for the financial health of the club.

When it came to the league, probably the best way to describe the way the season was going would be to say it was unremarkable. We'd played quite well and by the time the final against Doncaster came around we were just above the half way mark. We had never looked in any real trouble following the first two months of the season, but at the same time there weren't too many people looking at us as promotion candidates.

I've had a few occasions in my career where my teams have gone on a bit of a run, like that first season with Cardiff when we just missed out in the play-offs, but the sequence of results Rovers were about to put together was probably even more remarkable.

We had seven league matches left starting with a trip to Mansfield and after winning that one 1-0 we beat Bury 2-0 at home two days later and then remained unbeaten in our next four games, drawing the first two and winning the other couple of matches. By the time the last game of the season at Hartlepool rolled around we were in seventh place and knew we actually had a chance of getting into the play-offs if we stayed there or did better. Stockport were a place behind us in the table, but had fallen away towards the end of the season and knew that they needed to win at Darlington, hoping that we were denied a victory at Hartlepool if they were to get into the play-off places. Just to add further interest to our match, Hartlepool knew that they had to win if they wanted to leapfrog Walsall and be promoted as champions.

We found ourselves 1-0 down at half-time against Hartlepool and everyone knew that the great little run we'd managed to put together could come to nothing. We also knew that despite their recent poor form, Stockport were a goal up at Darlington. I've mentioned before that I think there are moments that can be life changing, and for our players the second half against Hartlepool turned out to be just that. After 14 minutes of the second half Richard Walker gave us a lifeline when he scored from the penalty spot and then right at the death, in the most dramatic fashion, we snatched victory with a goal from Rickie Lambert, which was the second of those two very significant goals. From looking nothing like promotion contenders for most of the season we'd done it and on the final day we'd got into sixth place ahead of Shrewsbury and Stockport, who missed out despite eventually beating Darlington 5-0. Our directors were delighted, not only had we made it into the play-offs, but sixth was the highest position the team had reached all season, and they only paid out bonuses if we were in the top six!

Coming off the sort of run we'd put together in the league, the team were absolutely flying when it came to the play-off semi-final against one of my old teams, Lincoln. They had finished a place above us in the table but we were all very confident that we could get past them over the two legs. We played them at home first and won 2-1, and our second leg performance was even better. As soon as we saw their pitch, which was immaculate, we knew we were going to be able to play well on it, and that's just what happened. We slaughtered them and won the match 5-3 to reach the final which was going to be played at Wembley. Our opponents and the team standing in our way were Shrewsbury, the same side we'd beaten on our way to the Johnstone's Paint Trophy final.

As well as the victory in that competition, we'd also won and drawn the two league games we had played against them, and I don't think they really fancied meeting us again. They went a goal up after just three minutes through Stuart Drummond, but I was sitting on the bench at Wembley feeling really confident. Don't ask me why, but it was one of those games where I just knew we were going to win. It happens from time to time, and I've been involved in quite a few matches over the years where I've had that same feeling and the result has gone the right way.

It did again that day at Wembley and two goals from Richard Walker gave us the lead at half-time. In a way we saved the best until last when we got a third in the final minute of the game. Understandably, Shrewsbury were throwing everything they could at us, and that included pushing their keeper, Chris MacKenzie, up for a corner. We cleared the ball and little Sammy Igoe picked it up and ran the length of the pitch with their keeper and defenders trying to get back. Sammy must have run 60 or 70 yards before finally rolling a shot into an empty goal, leaving a Shrewsbury defender desperately trying to stop the ball as he slid into the goal netting. We won 3-1 to make it an unforgettable day.

Not only had we been promoted, but in one season as a League Two side we'd been to the Millennium Stadium, Wembley Stadium and reached the fourth round of the FA Cup. In the process we had made between £1 million and £1.5 million. Nobody in the history of the game in this country has made as much coming out of the bottom division of the English leagues.

19

A CUP THAT CHEERS

It was a remarkable achievement for everyone concerned with the club and obviously great for Paul Trollope and me in our first full season together. To have made that much money and to get promotion, as well as have all the excitement of the Trophy and play-off finals, marked the season down as something special for the club and its fans.

Two days after the play-off win at Wembley the team were driven through the streets of Bristol in an open top bus, and the fans turned out in big numbers to welcome us back and cheer the players, although I was left behind at the reception. There were two buses that took us there and apparently the people in charge of each of them thought I was on the other. I ended up having to get a taxi back! But the reception was a great way to round things off for us and it wasn't too long before our thoughts turned towards the new season and the challenge of playing and competing at a higher level.

The players had put together a superb run to take us into the play-off and the success at the tail end of that season continued when we started the new campaign. We were unbeaten in our first five league matches before coming unstuck against Leeds in a home game, and then our league form suffered a little as we came to terms with the new division. It wasn't a disaster, but we struggled at home and had to wait until the middle of November before we recorded our first win in front of our own supporters, when we beat Millwall 2-1.

The week before that we'd started our FA Cup campaign with a first round tie at Leyton Orient, who were second in our league and playing very well. Like all of the sides in the bottom two divisions of the Football League, we began playing in the FA Cup in November, aiming to get through the first and second round so that we could be in the draw with the big boys of the Championship and Premier League when the third round was played in January.

In fact, Cup matches had been on the menu pretty early in the season for us when we played Crystal Palace from the Championship at home in the first round of the Carling Cup three days after the season had opened. It was a good test against a team playing in the division above us and after going a goal down in the first half, we came back to equalise after the break through Craig Disley and the game went into extra-time. The real drama came at the end of the added 30 minute period with the match still deadlocked at 1-1, because we had to go into a penalty shoot-out which we won 4-1. I didn't realise it at the time, but penalty drama in Cup games was to figure quite prominently in our season.

That win earned us a tie against Premier League West Ham United, who were managed by Alan Curbishley at the time. They had a bit too much for us with Craig Bellamy getting two first half goals for them before Andy Williams got one back for us, but we did well against them and there was a crowd of almost 11,000 to watch the match, which once again was important to the club financially.

By the time we prepared to travel to London for the game with Orient, we had also been knocked out of the Johnstone's Paint Trophy, so there was no chance of repeating the previous season's run. We knew that the game against the Londoners would be tough and had already lost to them in a home league match, when we were beaten 3-2 after being two goals up. Wayne Gray gave them the lead in the Cup game after 16 minutes and it looked as though we were on our way out, but with nine minutes of the match remaining a diving header from Rickie Lambert produced the equaliser and the chance to take them back to our place for the replay.

The second game suffered a postponement because of a water-logged pitch and by the time it was actually played, both teams knew that the winner would face a home tie against non-league Rushden & Diamonds, so on paper a win in the replay would give either Orient or ourselves a real chance to make it through to the third round draw.

The replay turned out to be a really exciting affair with end to end action and some refereeing decisions that had a lot of people puzzled. It was 1-1 at half-time, 2-2 at full-time and 3-3 at the end of extra-time. Add to that the fact that they finished the 120 minutes with nine men, and you get some idea of just how entertaining it must have been to watch. It was another penalty shoot-out with all the drama they bring. At one stage it was 4-3 to them and when Sammy Igoe stepped up to try and level things his kick was saved. I think most people thought that was going to be it for us, but there were more twists to come. Paul Terry had his kick saved by our keeper, Steve Phillips, who was a good shot-stopper and Craig Hinton levelled things for us at 4-4. On it went and after Adam Chambers hit the bar with his shot, Disley whacked home another penalty for us to make sure we won it 6-5. A crazy night and four days later we were back at the Memorial Stadium for the second round tie against Rushden.

There was no high drama this time and we ran out comfortable 5-1 winners, although we did go behind in the game before taking control. We'd made it into the third round and when you're in League One the thing you hope for at that stage is to get drawn in a money spinning tie against one of the Premier League big boys. That didn't quite happen for us, although we were handed a tie against a Premier League side. It wasn't Manchester United, Chelsea, Liverpool or Arsenal, but it was Fulham who were having a tough season in the league. By the time we travelled to London for the game in early January, along with 7,000 Rovers fans who made the journey east, Fulham had parted company with Lawrie Sanchez and had appointed Roy Hodgson as their manager. They were one off the bottom of the Premier League table and had just been beaten at home by their local rivals, Chelsea, five days earlier. If we were going to cause an upset against them I knew we'd probably never have a better chance. It was the first time I'd ever been up against Roy professionally and I knew that because he'd only just arrived at the club, the Fulham players would be out to impress their new boss. I also knew that Roy was tactically one of the most astute managers in the game, and that if anyone was equipped to sort the West London club out, it was him.

Our fans that day were fantastic occupying the whole of one end of the ground and singing their heads off throughout the game. It was played on a Sunday afternoon at 2pm, the day after most of the other ties had taken place. We had our captain, Stuart Campbell, suspended so we had to rearrange things in midfield, but the players enjoyed the occasion and worked their socks off throughout the game. We got the perfect start with a goal after just three minutes from Danny Coles and although David Healy equalised for them five minutes before the break, Craig Hinton sent our travelling fans wild 20 minutes into the second-half when he gave us the lead. That lasted until 17 minutes from time, when Danny Murphy got their second, but we'd got a draw and the chance to give it another go.

Once again the replay had to be postponed because our pitch was water-logged, so by the time the second game took place we knew that the winners would be travelling to play at Barnet four days later in the fourth round. Despite the game being given the go-ahead to be played, Fulham weren't too happy with our pitch.

To be honest, you had to have some sympathy with them because it wasn't in the best of conditions and every team that came to play us was wary of it. In the league it was a hindrance, but in the Cup it helped us. That night we had to battle hard not just for 90 minutes, but for another 30 after that and once again we were into the penalty shoot-out scenario. We deserved the draw and the team had put an awful lot into the tie, over both games. We scored from our first penalty and then Jimmy Bullard stepped up to the spot for them to take their first kick. Steve Phillips showed once more how good he was at saving spot kicks, as he kept the shot out and gave us an advantage. All of our lads scored and when the fifth one went in there was no need for Fulham to take their last kick, because it wouldn't have made a difference, we'd got through 5-3. It was the third time that season we had won a Cup match on penalties and all of them had come against opposition from London.

After all the excitement of winning the game it was important that we didn't lose sight of the fact that we were going to be facing Barnet just a few days later for a place in the fifth round. It was also important that we didn't lose sight of the fact that we had started to have a better time in the league with three wins and two draws, which had helped take us up the table from 20th spot into 16th place. Having a good Cup run was great for everyone, but the old saying about the league being a club's bread and butter is very true, particularly for us, and having worked so hard to get promotion the previous season we didn't want the Cup to distract us. We needed to make sure we consolidated in League One and continued to make progress as a club.

A goal from Rickie Lambert was enough to win the game at Barnet and as we prepared on the following Monday for a trip to Crewe the next night, the draw for the fifth round was made handing us a home tie against Southampton. It was a match against a side who were not having the best of times in the Championship, and having lost manager George

Burley who had taken the Scotland job, they had John Gorman and former Saints player, Jason Dodd, in temporary charge. The BBC obviously felt there might be an upset on the cards because they chose to screen it live as their lunchtime FA Cup game. Once again the crowd were superb making so much noise throughout the match and at half-time with the game goalless there was a real sense that we could go on and win it. As time went on after the break it looked more likely that we would have to go to the south coast for a replay, but with six minutes remaining we got a free kick outside their penalty area and Rickie Lambert's shot took a bit of a deflection before going into the net. Having scored it never looked as though the match had another goal in it, and when the final whistle blew Rovers were into the sixth round for the first time in 50 years.

The place understandably went wild and it was great for Trolls to be able to write his name into a little bit of club history. Getting into the quarter-finals was another great achievement and although I don't think anybody had any realistic hopes of going on to win the thing, it was realistic to think that if we got through the next round we would be at Wembley, because that's where the semi-finals were going to be played. The semi-final, if we reached it, would be our final because of everything that went with it in terms of taking fans to the match and the revenue the club could expect from such a game. We soon found out that in order to get that to happen we would have to get past another Championship side, West Bromwich Albion. Unlike Southampton who were struggling, Albion were flying at the top end of the table and were fourth when they came to the Memorial Stadium in March to play the sixth round game.

We found it very hard to handle their striker, Ishmael Miller, who ended up getting a hat-trick, and they were two up before Danny Coles gave us some hope of getting back into the game, but in the second half they scored three more times and ended up as 5-1 winners. We'd put a lot into a great Cup run but came up short at the final hurdle. Nevertheless, it had been one hell of a ride for everyone connected with the club, and would go down as another exciting season for Rovers.

So in two years we'd reached the fourth round of the FA Cup, the final of the Johnstone's Paint Trophy, won a play-off final at Wembley, beaten Palace and had a close game with West Ham in the Carling Cup and then gone all the way to the sixth round in the FA Cup. For a club of our size and considering where we were when Paul and I started working with each other, I think it was tremendous.

It also meant the club continued to take in much-needed revenue and I estimate that in two seasons we made something between £2 million and £3 million, it may not go too far when it comes to paying Cristiano Ronaldo's wages at Real Madrid, but it meant an awful lot to Bristol Rovers and the future of the club.

In more recent times Nick Higgs has taken over as the club's chairman and he has continued to be very supportive. Like the rest of us he knows how important it is to move on with things like a new stadium development, but these things don't happen overnight and there has to be the finances in place to support the effort.

It is inevitable for a club of Rovers' size that successful players are always going to attract interest, and that's exactly what happened with Rickie Lambert. In the end he was sold to Southampton in August 2009 for a fee in excess of £1 million and although they were a club in the same league as ourselves, they had the financial clout to be able to double his wages. Once a player becomes aware of that sort of offer there is very little we can do. But Rickie did a great job for Rovers and although you never want to lose your best players, when it becomes obvious that is what's going to happen, the most important thing is to get the best deal for the club, which is exactly what we did.

20

TWO'S COMPANY

It's very easy to look at football management and think it should purely and simply be about winning trophies, but the reality is very different. For a start only a handful of clubs win leagues and cups each season, so if trophies were the sole criteria on which you judged managers there would be very few who would be deemed successful.

In my book successful and effective football management is about a lot more than silverware. Of course it's great to win cups and finish at the top of a league, but when you look at the number of clubs there are playing professional football and at the resources, or lack of them, that so many have to operate within, it's clear that the job has to be about a lot more than trophies.

Unfortunately, fans, chairmen and boards of directors don't always see it that way. They are looking for instant success. Not all of them, but that trend is a lot more in evidence now than it has been before. There has always been pressure on managers, it's part of the job and if you're not prepared for it, then it's probably a good idea to get other employment. But at the same time I don't think it has ever been harder for a young manager coming into the job these days. The statistics for people who get sacked and don't get a second chance are scary.

That was something I was acutely aware of when I went to Rovers and began working with Paul. He was only just starting out as a manager, and I genuinely believe that any young manager needs a good support network around him if he is going to have a chance to grow into the job and go on to have a career. A manager needs all the help he can get in order to prolong his period of employment, especially with your first club.

Since getting his chance at Bristol Rovers when he was just 33, Paul has been moving the club in the right direction and I like to think I have played my part in making that happen. Although Rovers have a great fan base, the fact of the matter is that the club are not swimming in money, and therefore anything we do has to take into consideration the financial limitations that clubs at our level have to operate under. We're lucky in as much as the board is made up of realistic people who also happen to be Rovers fans. They want the best for their club but are sensible enough to know you don't get instant success, it needs to be built over a period of time and I also believe that continuity plays its part.

It was no coincidence that during a period of 24 years Charlton went from near relegation to the old Second Division in that first season I was in charge, to becoming an established Premier League side in 2006, when Alan Curbishley left them. During that entire period they only ever had two managers, although Curbs did the job alongside Steve Gritt for four seasons when he started out. The point is that the club as a whole benefited from gradual growth during that time and their belief in sticking with the manager. Since first teaming up in 2005 I have tried to help Trolls gradually improve not just the team, but also Bristol Rovers as a club because I see that as part of my brief.

In the first season the team finished half way in League Two. In the second season we got promotion and played at the Millennium and Wembley. In the third season, our first in League One, we had that great FA Cup adventure and eventually finished 16th in the table. Last season we ended up in 11th and at one stage it looked as though we might have an outside chance of perhaps putting a run together and snatching a play-off place. During all of this period the club have made a lot of money.

Lennie Lawrence

To many people all of the above may not sound earth shattering, but to anyone who really knows what the game is about, and who realises just how hard football management can be, they are facts and figures they will appreciate.

My partnership with Paul has worked well and during our time together I have enjoyed my role as director of football with Rovers. People often ask me about the job and how it works for me and the club. I've even had other chairmen phoning me up to discuss the role and they have asked how I go about it and why it has seemed to work so well for us. I don't think there's any doubt that it has worked for me and Trolls, but the fact is that there are no cast iron guarantees that it would work the same way at other clubs.

For a start, you don't normally get a director of football sitting on the bench, but I'm hands-on in the way I go about the job, and it was good that Paul wanted me in the dug-out from the very first day. I've mentioned that in order for a partnership like ours to work and flourish, the manager has to want to embrace the concept and then help evolve it. I think it has helped that although I am director of football, I have been a manager. I have been there, seen it and done it. Whatever Paul goes through in the job, I know exactly what he's feeling and can emphasise with him. The skill is to assist the manager without interfering and jeopardising the relationship. I think the whole thing works better with a younger manager, but I still think a director of football can work with a more experienced manager as long as he is prepared to embrace it.

A manager has got to look at you and think, 'he can help me'. I also think that for the job to work well the director of football has to be a real football man. Certainly at the level I'm operating at. I know bigger clubs have had directors of football who are chiefly concerned with recruitment and are basically operating as European scouts. There have been other terms and titles used by clubs such as technical director, or sports director. For me a technical director would be someone involved in all aspects of football at a football club, the youth policy, recruitment, and perhaps coaching up to, and perhaps including, first team level. A sports director is somebody whose main job would be player recruitment, contracts and negotiations when it comes to transfers. Certainly that would probably be the model they would look for on the continent. I think the director of football can be somewhere in between all of that. I've seen job descriptions for a director of football that would really need two or three people in order to carry out all the duties and functions they're asking for.

I see a classic director of football role as someone who generally oversees the whole football operation of a club. He can advise the manager, oversee the youth academy and medical operation, assist in the coaching if necessary and be part of the management team. Recruitment would also be part of the remit, but not the main part of it. I think the role has suffered in recent years because it has failed in a few high profile cases, but that doesn't mean there isn't a place for it in our game or that it can't work.

The key thing for any director of football is the relationship with the manager or coach, if it's not right it will never work. I like my involvement with the first team at Rovers, but it's a high skill to have that involvement and not interfere. To have the trust and respect of the manager without him thinking that you are after his job, you have to build a relationship.

The good thing was that I was ready for the role and it seemed to click from day one. Of course, you have good spells and bad spells, but happily the relationship between Trolls and me has never been under threat. Whether that's luck, hard work or the right attitude from both of us I don't know. Maybe it's a combination of all three things. I believe that during the course of the time we have worked together there have been a couple of occasions where my advice has proved to be crucial in helping him do his job. Fate threw us together and it has worked out and perhaps the fact that it has might prompt other clubs to look at the possibilities. I certainly think it might be easier for a partnership like ours to work lower down the leagues rather than at the very top. Ultimately in order for me to do my job well I have to understand the workings of a football club and I have to be able to deal with people right through that football club.

I have been in the game a long time and understand managers and management. I'm often asked what people coming into the profession should do when they start out, so here goes. Let me give you a few thoughts on the manager's manual according to Lennie!

I believe it is vitally important when you become a manager to have a contrast of people and personalities on your staff. What you don't want or need are all the same type of people. You might have someone working for you who is a bit abrasive, or someone else who can put an arm around a player and have a quiet word if it's needed, maybe somebody who is old and another person who is young, but the one thing they must all have in common is the fact that they must be of the right quality. A golden rule to remember is that first class people appoint first class people, second class people appoint third class people.

There's no ready made formula when it comes to being a manager and being able to make a go of it. I'm a great believer in qualifications, but they are not the be all and end all of the job, they can help you prepare for what it entails. You can do the C, B and A licences which are basically coaching qualifications, which will also address some aspects of management. There is also the League Managers Association, who run courses at the University of Warwick for players who are coming to the end of their careers and perhaps are thinking of staying on in the game as managers. It's very useful and looks at all aspects of the job, including things like media training, the need for which has become so much greater in the modern game. Then there is the pro-licence which again deals with coaching, but also all aspects of management including things like psychology, preparation and time management. I believe anyone coming into the profession who is genuinely serious about the job should have done all of these courses and qualifications by the time they are 40.

In places like Italy and Spain you can't even get a job without the right qualifications. In theory that is also the case in the Premier League, but in recent years that has not been a hard and fast rule. I have no problem with exceptions being made for some managers, but I do think that anyone getting a job in the Premier League who is under 45 should have the right qualification or at least be working towards it to show intent and the fact that they are serious about the job.

We have the ridiculous situation in the Football League where there is no mandatory qualification. In theory an owner of a club in League Two could give the manager's job to the milkman if he wanted to, and that milkman could then give the assistant manager's job to the baker. It's crazy and I think it does nothing for the integrity of the job or the fact that you have to be highly professional in order to do it well.

The most important quality for a manager is intelligence because the job is so diverse, so demanding and so hard these days. There is never a guarantee that someone who becomes a manager will be a success and be able to cope with the demands of the job. Sometimes there are people coming to the end of their careers who you think fit the bill and yet they're not up to it. Other people who you might not think are suited to the task, come through and do really well. Certainly playing success doesn't mean you are naturally going to be a good manager.

Someone who has played at the very top will always have the initial respect of the players if he becomes a manager, but the fact of the matter is that if you can't coach or manage players, if they are not learning anything from your coaching or your management is not getting the best out of them as a team, then that respect soon goes out of the window. When I took my first coaching session at Plymouth all those years ago, I knew I had to make an impression. In my own case all I really wanted to do to begin with was coach. I had a good apprenticeship at both Plymouth and Lincoln, so when the opportunity came along at Charlton to take over from Ken Craggs, I was ready and the experiences I had there fashioned me as a manager. I always ask potential managers, are you a manager who can coach, or a coach who can manage? Some people drift into it and don't really know what they are or what they're doing. You see some people grow in stature and relish the job, while others appear to shrink from it and end up looking like a rabbit caught in headlights.

As a manager you go into work each day knowing there is going to be a different problem. Sometimes the problem is big, sometimes it's small and sometimes there is more than one problem to deal with. I very quickly began to enjoy the diversity that brought and I relish the variety of the job because you never know what is going to happen. Someone once said to me that you should make a problem into an opportunity and in many ways that's what I've been doing all my life in management.

Man management is also an important ingredient of the job. You can do what you like with players throughout the week in terms of coaching, tactics and training, but they have to want to go out on a Saturday and play for you. They can play for the club and the shirt and their family and friends. All of that, but they have to want to play for the manager.

Obviously the pressure, expectation and money involved in the game is greater than ever, and things like the January transfer window and the power of fans have had an effect. The window often dictates the thinking of a chairman or board of directors, they think from window to window and it just puts extra pressure on the manager. Fans have never had a greater weight of opinion. The average fan can be standing behind the dug-out at the end of a match screaming abuse, at 5pm he can be phoning in to his local radio station, he can text into the 606 programme on national radio and then go home and send emails to websites! The point I'm trying to make is that there have never been more media outlets at the disposal of the average supporter. Ideally a manager needs steadiness, a calm environment and continuity. The media needs drama, change and speculation. It's all part of the game and you have to be able to get on with it.

One aspect of the job that has changed since I first became a manager is the lack of opportunity at the really big clubs for English managers, and I think it is a real shame. A few years after I started off in the professional game Dave Sexton parted company with Manchester United. They gave the job to Ron Atkinson who had done very well with West Bromwich Albion, and he got the chance to manage one of the biggest clubs in the world. That simply would not happen today. I know Alan Curbishley well and know the qualities he had as a player and a manager. He did a fantastic job with Charlton, and I know how hard that was, but he never once got the chance of taking over at one of the really big clubs when there were vacancies, which is staggering really and very disheartening for English managers. With very few exceptions, you have to take a club into the Premier League in order to get a chance to work in it.

Foreign managers and coaches have done very well in England, with people like Arsène Wenger showing just what a great manager and coach he is, while the likes of José Mourinho and Rafael Benitez have also won trophies, but I'm not certain the quality and depth of the foreign manager is any greater than English managers. English managers don't get the chance. It's a vicious circle when it comes to the big jobs. They don't have the experience of managing at that level because they don't get the opportunity, and they don't get the opportunity because they don't have the experience. It does seem a shame and I would love to see that trend change, but I don't hold out much hope.

Having said all of that I still believe management is a fantastic profession to be part of and that football is a wonderful industry to be involved in. I first got the chance to coach and manage way back in 1977 and I'm still around and working in 2009. That's 32 years doing a job I absolutely love which is something most people can only dream of – what a lucky boy I am!

ACKNOWLEDGEMENTS

It was only when I began the process of writing this book that I realised just how many people have played a part in my life story. It is inevitable that some names and instances have slipped from my memory, and for that I apologise. I have had a tremendous life as a footballing man and I realise that without the help and assistance of so many people along the way, this just would not have been possible.

There are so many people I want to say thank you to, and I make no apologies for producing possibly one of the longest lists of acknowledgements ever published in a book of this kind! Some of the names mentioned are no longer with us, but I feel it is fitting that I should try to pay tribute and say thanks in my own way for helping to make my life so rewarding and interesting. Despite my efforts I have no doubt that there will still be some people I have missed out, and for that let me say sorry in advance. But I hope that if they know me, and have been involved in my life, they will recognise just where they fit into the story I have tried to tell.

Anyone reading this book will know what a huge part Charlton Athletic played in the story and for that reason I think it is appropriate that I start with them and some of the people who were of huge significance during my time there.

In no particular order I would like to say thanks to former secretary Graham Hortop for his experience, advice and calmness in the most troubled of times, to Anne Payne, who was a Charlton supporter through and through and who helped me during some difficult times as part of a small and loyal group of staff at The Valley. To Brian Eastick, for his coaching ability, and contribution during the memorable play-off victory over Leeds, to Peter Eustace, for being a good coach and having such a down-to-earth approach to the game, and to Mike Flanagan, who was a talented coach who helped us significantly during the early years in the old Division One and also served as a player who was sheer quality on the pitch. To Les Gore for giving me the benefit of his vast experience during afternoon sessions over a cup of tea at The Valley when everyone else had gone home, and to Charlie Hall for his experience and for being such a help during my early years in management. I also want to thank physio Bill Gallagher, who always had his ear to the ground, Eddie Heath, for his recruitment skills and fantastic contacts in youth football, Roy Passey, a highly regarded schoolboy and youth coach and Eddie May, who was my first appointment as assistant manager and someone with a strong personality who was a massive help early on. A very special thanks must go to Arnie Warren, who was my most significant appointment at Charlton. He was a huge influence on me as a manager and I cannot speak highly enough of him for his mentoring during my early years as manager of the club. He was not only knowledgeable and experienced when it came to professional football, he was also like a second father to me. I am certain I could not have got through many situations without his presence and advice.

There were also many people in the background at the club who did tremendous jobs on a regular basis and were part of the fabric of Charlton during the time I was there. One of them was Peter Burrowes, a journalist who was press officer and programme editor. He was an essential part of Charlton folklore and I'm sure has more than a tale or two of his own to tell about his time with the club. Audrey Hannant was a totally loyal supporter and a lovely woman for whom nothing was too much trouble. Carol Harris was another tireless worker in the background at the club, as was Geraldine Salter, who was fundamental to the place.

And then there was big Paul Pace, or 'Maltese Paul' who although was not part of the official Charlton administration, seemed to always be at the ground and at all of our matches. As far as the players and staff were concerned, you always knew you were in safe hands when Paul was around. Colin Cameron was, and still is, a wonderful stats man, who has given me invaluable help and was an integral part of putting this section of the book together.

I also want to acknowledge the role played by Ken Craggs in my career. He gave me the job of reserve team coach in the summer of 1982, which in turn signalled the start of my Charlton story. I also have to thank Mark Hulyer for giving me his backing and Alan Ward for his support as a director in the early part of my Charlton career and for his ongoing friendship. John Fryer for supporting me as manager, and more especially, for financially backing me in the transfer market as I assembled a team to get us promotion in 1986. I also need to mention Jimmy Hill for his help during the time he was acting chairman of the club when he gave me advice and support as I began recruiting those players.

Roger Alwen and Mike Norris need a special mention for picking up the baton from John Fryer and Sunleys, taking Charlton to the next stage by purchasing and developing our own training ground and setting the club on a path that would eventually see them return to The Valley, and for supporting me whenever possible in the transfer market. Roger Alwen is one of the best men I have ever met in football, and in life. Without his contribution Charlton Athletic could not have progressed as a club in the way that they did. I would also like to pay tribute to Richard Murray and Martin Simons who appeared on the scene towards the end of my time at the club, but who went on to play huge roles in making Charlton so successful. Thanks also to Richard Collins, a director before I got to The Valley, throughout my time there and also after I had left. He's given unstinting support to the club and helped me during my time as manager. I would also like to pay a special tribute to Derek Ufton, a director who was a fantastic football man, and someone who belonged to that dying breed of sportsmen who reached the top of their profession playing both football and cricket. He's a wonderful man and along with his wife, Judy, their humility, warmth and kindness provided a huge source of support to me.

I also want to put on record my thanks to Alan Curbishley and Steve Gritt for their work in very difficult circumstances as they picked up the reigns after I left the club. The pair had been terrific players with the club and had done good jobs as coaches. When I left they took joint control of the team and for four years worked as a partnership as the club finally returned to The Valley. In 1995 Curbs took sole charge and everyone now knows that he went on to become a highly successful manager, who guided the club into the Premier League and established them in the top flight.

It is fitting to thank all of those players who wore the Charlton badge during my time with the club, in what were unique times. Players like Derek Hales who provided so many goals and who did such a great job in helping us to stay up in my first season. Robert Lee who emerged as a great young talent and went on to have a fantastic career. I want to thank stalwarts like Nicky Johns and Les Berry, as well as Mark Aizlewood who provided great leadership in our promotion season and went from being a club reject to club captain. To Peter Shirtliff, one of the best half dozen buys of my career, who was a real 'Captain Fantastic' for me, to Paul Miller for great leadership and character in helping us to fight relegation, we had our ups and downs during the time I managed him, but he has my utmost respect, and also to Garth Crooks for some vital goals during his time with the club.

Thanks also to Bob Bolder, a great character and goalkeeper who was enormously popular, and Andy Peake who is one of the few players I have signed twice, to the much maligned Carl Leaburn who received criticism when he came into the side as a youngster, but who showed great character and proved what a terrific team player he was. Colin Walsh was an outstanding player for me and a great footballer who was really appreciated by the Charlton supporters, and John Humphrey who was also one of my six best ever buys. I must also mention Mark Reid who was a marvellous full-back, Steve Thompson, a unique character and leader and George Shipley, who I later took to Bradford as an assistant and who did a good job as youth coach with Middlesbrough. I also want to thank Alan Mullery for his time and help with some of the details concerning the club that I joined all of those years ago, and a special thanks to all of those people who worked at Charlton Athletic when the very existence of the club was at stake.

At Middlesbrough I want to thank chairman Colin Henderson, chief executive Keith Lamb, as well as directors Graham Fordy and Reg Corbidge for giving me the chance to work at a fantastic football club; my assistant John Pickering who was loyal, honest, hard working and unbelievably popular with the players. He is without doubt one of the best men I have ever met in my life. I also want to thank some of the outstanding players I had during my time at Middlesbrough. People like Tony Mowbray for his captaincy and leadership in that first season, Alan Kernaghan who later became captain and was a massive influence, Paul Wilkinson, an outstanding striker and someone who I went on to work with at Cardiff as part of my coaching staff. We've had a great professional relationship, and also a friendship for many years now. Bernie Slaven for his goals and contribution, despite our up and down relationship; Graham Kavanagh who made his debut under me and who also played for me at Cardiff;

Robbie Mustoe, John Hendrie, a fantastic personality and a big part of our promotion season, and Stephen Pears, the best keeper in England bar none during that promotion season. Also, backroom staff Norman Hardy, with whom I have maintained a friendship over the years, thanks to Jane Woods, Diane O'Connell and Karen Nelson who have worked there all their adult lives, for their support.

I want to thank Geoffrey Richmond at Bradford for appointing me, even though we both realised after a very short period of time that we perhaps weren't right for each other. My thanks also to Alan 'Gilly' Gilliver, Mr Bradford, for his unfailing support and good humour during my time at the club, and he remains a good friend to this day, and to Chris Kamara for his support as player-coach at the club during my time there, and for carrying on the good work after I left by leading the club to promotion.

I want to thank David Kohler for appointing me at Luton and also his board of directors at the time. I want to thank Cliff Bassett for his friendship and support during some difficult times that might have seen me leave the club earlier than I did. My thanks also go to Cherry Newbery, because without her my job at Luton would have been made even more difficult. She gave tremendous loyalty and service to Luton and only recently ended a very long and distinguished career with them. I had some great lads playing for me during my time at Kenilworth Road, and I'd like to thank Tony Thorpe for his record goals that got us into the play-offs, Marvin Johnson, Gary Waddock, Steve Davis, and to all the young players at Luton who carried the flag for the club and acted like men despite really being no more than boys. To Matty Taylor, Emmerson Boyce, Matthew Upson, Gary Doherty. Thanks also to Wayne Turner, an excellent coach, Trevor Hartley, a great coach and chief scout, and also John Moore, a one club man who did a fantastic job for Luton over many years as well as for me during my time at the club, and whose Christian values managed to remain intact despite working in the ruthless world of football.

At Grimsby I want to thank Brian Huxford and the late Doug Everitt for appointing me to the job of manager at a very friendly club who battled to stay in the Championship and gave me a very exciting and happy first year with them. My thanks to John Cockerill, a player and coach who was also my assistant and was caretaker manager at the club, he gave me invaluable support during my time there.

I want to thank Sam Hammam for appointing me at Cardiff, to Alan Cork for his professionalism, maturity and understanding during and after his time at the club. Chief executive David Temme for his endless support in dealing with various problems, and for his work towards a new stadium which has happily now come to fruition; I also want to thank Steve Borley, a Cardiff director for many years and a very knowledgeable man when it came to the game. Thanks to Michael Isaac for his loyal support and enthusiasm, an entertaining man who is always good company and has remained a good friend. He also lent invaluable financial support that saw Cardiff through one of the most difficult periods in their history. I also want to thank some outstanding players who were at Cardiff during my time with them, some of whom went on to play Premier League football; people like Graham Kavanagh, Danny Gabbidon, James Collins, Robert Earnshaw – one of the best strikers in the penalty area I've worked with – lads like Scott Young, Peter Thorpe, and Andy Legg for his contribution on and off the pitch. Thanks to Matthew Crocker for helping to set up the academy at the club and to my staff, Ian Butterworth, Clive Goodyear, George Wood, who kept my spirits up in difficult times and, of course, Terry Burton, an outstanding coach who was very influential during the time we worked together. A special thanks to Jason Turner, referred to by mutual friends as the son I never had, he's a great club secretary, the hardest working man in the world who always shows great professionalism, and he is also a friend and confidant.

My thanks to the directors at Bristol Rovers, led at the time by Geoff Dunford, the chairman, who had the courage and foresight to appoint a director of football alongside a young coach, and who have given the idea their support and time for us to develop the club. Thanks to Nick Higgs, the current chairman, for allowing the club to progress and supporting the status quo during some often turbulent times. My thanks also to the hard working staff at the club whose contribution in the 2006-07 season helped produce a quite unprecedented time for the club; thanks to Ian Holtby, 'Mr Bristol Rovers', for his unfailing hard work and support, nothing is too much trouble for Ian, kit man Roger Harding, Keith Brookman, a man of many jobs who never walks but always runs, physios Phil Kite and Steve Bissix, club secretary Rod Wesson for great help and support, and to all the staff at Rovers, not least an ever improving group of players, including the likes of Stuart Campbell, Chris Lines, Stevie Elliott and Aaron Lescott. Thanks also to Rickie Lambert for his contribution while he was at the club. I would also like to thank Paul Trollope, a fine young man and a talented coach who will develop into an excellent manager, he bravely embraced the idea of working with a director of football and we have a personal and professional relationship that has gone from strength to strength. He is very much his own man and I truly believe he is destined to have a long and successful career in the game.

There are some great friends who have played a part in my life and in no particular order, I would like to thank them for being part of my story. Bobby Houghton, a lifelong friend, who has spent virtually all his career abroad, and whose interest in coaching helped inspire me. Roy Hodgson, another lifelong friend and in my opinion one of the best 20 coaches in the world, he was a huge influence on me and like Bobby, an inspiration.

Lennie

Colin Toal who was involved in the coaches' set-up with me from way back and who is someone I have maintained a friendship with, despite him working around the globe during a tremendous career. Ray Buckley, for a shared involvement in football and someone who has been a valued friend who has given me sound advice. To Barry Simmonds, professional colleague and a good friend over the last 10 years, whose knowledge and contacts helped enormously. My thanks to Mike Kelly for giving me my first job in professional football, without which my career may never have got started, and this book never written! Thanks also to Malcolm Allison for his coaching advice, allowing me to pick his brains and for his tolerance working with someone who was so young and inexperienced at the time. To the Plymouth chairman at the time, Robert Daniel and vice-chairman Peter Skinnard, I could not have been given a better start, and I learned a lot from them with regard to the roles of managers and directors at football clubs. At Lincoln I was very lucky to work with Colin Murphy, who knocked all the rough edges off of me and gave me the chance to understand what management was all about and without him I might have sunk without a trace. It was a great experience which helped me prepare for what was to come at Charlton. I also want to thank all of those at Carshalton many years ago for giving me the chance to coach. A special mention goes to Sir Alex Ferguson who was kind enough to take the time and trouble to provide the foreword for this book. He is not only a great manager but also a great man and it has been a genuine privilege to have known him and enjoyed his friendship for so many years.

Thanks to Frank Allen and his wife Jackie. Quite simply, Frank is my best friend and has been for years. He's given me fantastic support and is a warm person whose help with the training ground when I was at Charlton was fantastic; to Bob Bevan, a long time friend who is always such great company, and who first suggested to me that it might be a good idea to write a book; thanks also to Dave Bassett, someone who has been a great friend and professional colleague over many years. I think I must have spoken to him concerning every major footballing decision in my life during the past 25 years. He's a totally different character to me, but we have always got on so well, and I hugely respect his advice. To The La Manga Crew. Every year for the past 25 years they have made sure I am not a football manager for a week! Thanks to Plater, Spawny, Herman, Flash, Frank, Walks, Hillsy, Perry, Burkey, Micky, Dennis (The Captain), Chuck, Clive and Cleggy 'The Organiser'.

I would like to thank publisher Vanessa Gardner, editor Becky Ellis, creative director Kevin Gardner and Ellie Charleston at Green Umbrella for their help and support.

Finally, a special thanks to Kevin Brennan who collaborated with me in the writing of this book and to his wife Lynda and children James and Rachel for putting up with us while working on the project.

Lennie Lawrence, August 2009